G000129070

Available Books by George Mikes

TSI-TSA
The Biography of a Cat

TSI-TSA

The Biography of a Cat

BY

George Mikes

* * *

Nicolas Bentley
drew the pictures

ANDRE DEUTSCH

First published 1978 by
André Deutsch Limited
105 Great Russell Street London WC1

Filmset in Imprint 101
by A. Brown & Sons Ltd Hull England

Printed in Great Britain by
Lowe & Brydone Printers Ltd
Thetford Norfolk

ISBN 0 233 97063 0

To Harry, an Errol Flynn;
to George, an Albert Einstein;
and to Ginger, a saint among cats.

Arrival

*   *   *

'WHAT'S this?' I asked Eva.

'A cat. A black cat.'

'I can see it's black.'

'Then why can't you see it's a cat?'

'What's this cat doing here?' I asked her as sternly as I can ask anything.

'Nothing in particular. What do cats do? It's a very nice cat.'

This remark puzzled me.

'What do you mean a *nice* cat? Aren't all cats the same? A cat is a cat.'

Eva threw me a glance in which contempt was mixed with pity. She did not think it worthwhile to explain or to argue.

*   *   *

The front door of our house, leading to the patio, is often kept open in warm weather. That little black cat went on appearing from time to time, making herself comfortable under the table or on an armchair. On one occasion, quite unexpectedly, she (I was informed that she was a female) jumped on my lap and settled down. I was surprised. This was quite a new

9

experience. What was I to do? I did not like to be impolite and throw her off; on the other hand I felt a bit silly, sitting there with a book in one hand and a cat on my lap. She fell alseep and I could not get up for nearly an hour.

The next time she came in I was again sitting in that same armchair, reading. I picked her up. She jumped off immediately and walked away, looking back with lofty disdain. The meaning of that look was quite clear: 'I'll sit on your lap when it suits *me* and not when you deign to pick me up. What d'you think I am? A dog?'

'Has Cica been in?' I asked Eva a few days later.

'Who's Cica?'

'*Cica* is the Hungarian word for *pussy*. As I don't know her name . . . Well, do *you*?'

'No, I don't. How do you spell *Cica*?'

'I spell it C-I-C-A but she, being English, would probably spell it Tsi-Tsa.'

'That sounds Chinese to me.'

'Never mind. Has she been in?'

'Are you missing her, by any chance?'

'Of course not. I couldn't care less. I am surprised that I remembered her at all. But she used to come regularly. Why isn't she coming now?'

'Because she's a cat. She comes when she feels like it.'

'Whose cat is she?' I asked.

'No idea. Hard to find out. She is, you see, the friendliest cat in Fulham. She visits everybody. I see her go in and out of all the houses, sitting in all the windows, playing in all the front-gardens. Everybody spoils her because she is so beautiful.'

'You keep saying that she is beautiful. What's beautiful in her? One cat is like another.'

I said it again, but with much less conviction.

*　　*　　*

I contemplated my relationship with animals. It did not come to much.

I was born in a large village (now a small town) in Hungary, called Siklós. I was surrounded by animals, consequently took no notice of them. There were chickens and geese in our back yard; horses in the streets – motorcars were still such rarities that when we children heard the roar of one, we rushed out to the street to watch. We lived in the centre of Siklós, its Piccadilly Circus, so cows did not go out at dawn and return at dusk with their bells ringing; but cows were, all the same, familiar features of the landscape.

Birds interested me more. We lived bang opposite the Town Hall which had a clock-tower. On the top of the tower lived, when in residence, a family of storks. I loved those birds, large, beautiful and dignified, and was always pleased to see them arrive. Their arrival meant the arrival of spring, too, of course, but I loved them for their own sake. They were fond of resting for a while on the large fingers of the town clock, pushing them down or else preventing them from rising. The municipal authorities occasionally decided that the face of the clock ought to be covered by glass, but it was never done. Everybody knew that in the summer the storks made the town clock a little fast (or slow) and that was that.

The storks, as I have said, lived on the Town Hall and they were the guests of the whole community.

We, in our own house, had a family of swallows. They came more or less at the same time as the storks, got busy rebuilding or redecorating their nest just under the doorway, brought pieces of mud and other building material in their beaks and later caught beautiful fat flies for their babies. They were part of the landscape, I acknowledged their existence as I acknowledged the existence of the chickens and the geese, but was not really interested in them – far less than I was in the storks. When later, in London, I heard the expression *birdwatching,* its meaning had to be explained to me. Who watches birds? And why? And why so early in the morning? When I met my first snail-watcher and saw him crawl around on all fours in a friend's garden for hours on end, I thought he was mad. I still do. I see the point in snail-watcher-watching. But in snail-watching? My father tried to arouse my interest by explaining that the swallows left for Africa in order to get away from our harsh winters, and returned with the good weather. Didn't I think this was wonderful? And didn't I think it miraculous that they could always find our little house in the small village of Siklós? No, I didn't think it miraculous at all. I had an Aristotelian turn of mind and thought in categories. The swallows – as it had been explained to

12

me – were migrating birds. What was so miraculous in migrating birds migrating? It would have been much more miraculous if migrating birds had failed to migrate. And what was so difficult in finding our house? I was a little boy, yet I never had any difficulty in finding it.

*　　*　　*

I had a painful encounter with a bird and its memory haunted me for years. Perhaps it still does.

I was going home from the Castle – the only historic building of Siklós, where a king had been imprisoned in the 15th century – and walking down the hill I noticed that an angry goose was approaching me, followed by a gaggle of goslings. I must have aroused her fear or suspicion – perhaps she was worried about her offspring – and she was coming towards me with determined steps, hissing furiously. I stopped for a moment but she did not; she came nearer and nearer and her hissing sounded more and more menacing. So I decided that we might as well part company. I took to my heels and ran away as fast as I could. The goose – a ferocious animal, smelling blood, and realising that I was afraid of her – started pursuing me, running faster and faster, hissing more and more fiercely. Suddenly I heard loud, mocking laughter. Two little peasant boys were watching the scene and scoffed at my running away from a goose.

For a long time I dreaded the thought that my friends might hear of this inglorious encounter. They never did. My dark secret has been revealed to the world here for the first time.

*　　*　　*

Among all animals the horses were nearest to my heart. They were large, sad, benevolent. Some pulled light carriages, others heavy carts, loaded with greed and callousness. Sometimes the horses could not move the carts, the wheels often sank axle-deep into the mud. The drivers used their whips freely, beating the horses with ferocious brutality, swearing loudly and angrily. The horses' backs were sore from previous beatings and now the blood started oozing out. Their pain must have been excruciating. They tried to pull the carts out of the mud, the effort of their stretched legs and whole, tormented bodies was desperate but the whip fell upon them whirring and swishing mercilessly. The drivers went on swearing, the horses went on bleeding and no passer-by turned a hair; no one was even looking. It was all part of life. The drivers had a job to do and this was the way they had always done it. Cruelty was not cruelty; it was life itself.

It was in those days, I think, that I developed a stronger than normal aversion to beating. My parents never beat me. No teacher or master ever touched me. I was involved in fights with other boys (not too often, I was neither violent nor brave enough) but, in any case, that was different: I could hit back, and tried to – even if more often unsuccessfully than not. The horse could not hit back. I am a rather quiet, perhaps even indolent person, but if anyone were to hit me nowadays – however strong a man, however well armed – I would hit him back, go for him, attack him and try to tear him to bits whatever the consequences. All this in revenge for the horses of Siklós.

*　　*　　*

14

And then Victor came into our lives.

My mother was a sweet, even-tempered, charming and muddle-headed young woman, always ready to laugh at her mishaps and little calamities. My father adored her and loved teasing her. She decided one day that we needed a new set of saucepans. She was not a thrifty person – quite the contrary – but occasionally she was determined to save on small purchases. Her endeavours to save usually proved expensive. Now she decided that she ought to buy the saucepans at the market. Market came to Siklós four times a year and it was quite a hullabaloo. Two or three streets were filled with tents. The vendors were mostly peasants, but there were also artisans among them and the funfair was run by crafty people from the neighbouring towns. My mother kept speaking of the new set of saucepans and, in the end, the whole family was looking forward eagerly to the next market day and the arrival of the new treasure.

My mother looked flushed, excited and happy when she came home from the market.

'Show me those famous saucepans,' said my father.

'I bought no saucepans,' my mother replied. 'I bought a *bikla* instead.'

Now *bikla* is a Hungarian word. Yet, ask a hundred Hungarians what it means and ninety-nine will never have heard it. I have two excellent Hungarian dictionaries, and neither of them includes it. Perhaps it is local dialect.

My father was a fourth-generation Siklós man, and *he* had never heard it either.

'What is a *bikla*?' he asked.

'A *bikla*,' my mother explained with a touch of

15

superiority in her voice, 'is a peasant skirt consisting of seven layers and worn on festive occasions, mostly at weddings.'

My father nodded.

'But what exactly did you mean, Margot darling, when you said that you bought this *bikla* instead of saucepans? How can it replace saucepans?'

'Did I say *instead*?'

'You did.'

'Hm . . . Well, I bought it *instead* in the sense that I spent the money allocated for the saucepans on the *bikla*.'

'And are you going to wear this peasant skirt of seven layers on festive occasions, for example at Magda Mautner's forthcoming wedding?'

'I am going to cut it up,' my mother replied somewhat coolly, 'and use the pieces for dusters and kitchen-cloths.'

'They would be extremely useful,' my father said, 'to clean saucepans with, if you had any saucepans.'

My mother explained that she would have to do without proper saucepans for a while. But once she had the saucepans she would need to have them cleaned with proper kitchen-cloths, wouldn't she? So the *bikla*-pieces were necessary, indeed essential. What difference did it make in what order she acquired these badly needed household goods? Whether she bought the saucepans first and the kitchen-cloths later or vice versa?

'You don't want,' my father asked, 'just to go to the shop and buy the saucepans at Mr Trenkert's?'

'No,' my mother said firmly and proudly. 'I will wait for the next market day.'

My brother and I, aged three and eight re-
spectively, were looking forward to the next market
day. The *bikla* was a good beginning. What was
mother going to buy instead of saucepans this time?

She bought a dog.

*   *   *

This time a tiny puppy, a mongrel of extremely varied
ancestry, was brought home instead of saucepans.
Fox terrier forefathers – among many others – were
clearly discernible. He was black with a white chest
and huge, flappy brown ears. My mother named him
Victor. It was never quite clear why Victor. We had
no Victor in the family, let alone one whom she liked
or disliked particularly. Perhaps he got the name
because he had defeated the saucepans.

We immediately fell in love with Victor. Yet, three
days later he was sentenced to death.

His crime was grave: he had bitten Tibor, my
younger brother. Victor was chewing a bone and
Tibor – three years old and not very experienced
with dogs – playfully tried to take it away from him.
Victor failed to see the joke, snapped at Tibor,

scratched his hand with his tiny teeth and drew blood. The doctor – an uncle of ours – was called in and Tibor walked about for a few days with some green ointment on his hand. My father decreed that Victor was to die. He could not possibly have a ferocious bloodhound in the house who went around mauling and maiming his sons and spreading rabies. He had called – we were told – Mr Sloboda, the dog-catcher, who would take Victor away and kill him. The house was plunged into utter gloom. Tibor looked pathetic with his green hand but he was more upset than anyone else because he felt responsible for Victor's doom. My mother was firmly on our side, partly because she, too, loved Victor, partly because Victor's ignominious exit as a child-murderer would have diminished the success of her purchase: no saucepan would have bitten anyone. By the evening my father relented a little: all right, Victor would not be given to Mr Sloboda but he would be given away. He definitely could not stay in the house. By next morning the partial reprieve became a full reprieve: Victor could stay. He got away with a stiff warning, administered in a very severe tone.

Victor grew up into a sweet, good-natured and very small dog. We never had to take Victor for a walk and never bought dog-food for him. He took himself for walks whenever he fancied and dog-food was not available in Siklós: he got the left-overs and throve on them. Only one further difficulty remained: he was a little slow to learn that he was not to chase the chickens in the back-yard. But Auntie Kati's expostulations, threats, shouts and occasional gentle beating with the soft end of a sweep made this rule clear. The chickens, once terrified of him, got used to his presence. Victor could walk around in their midst, lie down and sun himself and they took no notice of their former ferocious enemy. But this idyllic, peaceful co-existence was misleading, as peaceful co-existence so often is. One day Auntie Kati appeared in the back-yard and saw the usual picture: Victor sunning himself, fast asleep and the chickens picking up grain around him, not paying him the slightest attention. Auntie Kati was our maid, an elderly Croatian peasant-woman, with a strong personality and a sharp tongue. My mother dreaded her, although our impression was that although Auntie Kati was always strict with Mother, she was also just. Sometimes Auntie Kati (or could it have been Mother? I doubt it) decided that we would have chicken for lunch. On such occasions the chicken had to be killed – an easy job for Auntie Kati – but in order to be killed it had to be caught first, a much more difficult task. We got used to the scene: Auntie Kati chasing a chicken, the whole brood fleeing and flying in all directions, flapping their wings, clucking hysterically while Auntie Kati swore loudly and angrily in the melodious Croatian tongue. She could frighten them all right, but she could not catch them without a long, long chase and even then never the one she meant to catch.

On this day Auntie Kati appeared in the back-yard and pointed at one of the chickens. Victor looked at Auntie Kati and his eyes seemed to reply: yes, he knew he was not allowed to chase them, he had done nothing wrong, he was simply lying here in the sun, his conscience was clear. But in the end, Victor – to his own amazement, no doubt – understood the signals: with one single leap he threw himself on the chicken, caught it and held it, without harming it, until Auntie Kati arrived, bent down in a leisurely manner, took it from Victor with an appreciative nod and carried it away to its inevitable doom. We witnessed this scene many times afterwards: Victor and the chickens peacefully enjoying life together for days, sometimes for weeks, and then, suddenly – when instructed – Victor catching and holding a chicken until she was taken away and killed. The chickens were killed one by one but somehow the friendship and trust between dog and chickens was never impaired. (When Khrushchev talked of peaceful co-existence in the late fifties and early sixties, he had something similar in mind.)

One day Victor disappeared. He just failed to turn up. Next day Father told us that he had been caught by the dog-catcher: as a puppy he had avoided Mr Sloboda's clutches but now he was caught for roaming the streets unaccompanied by a human and – obviously – not on a lead. No dog of Siklós ever walked on a lead and few were accompanied, but the regulations existed and were occasionally, if somewhat whimsically, enforced. Father was to pay a stiff fine, otherwise Victor would be destroyed. At first Father refused to pay, but later, needless to say, he succumbed to our entreaties and was defeated by the unalleviated gloom that descended upon the house. A frightened but happy, even triumphant, Victor was re-united with the family, ransomed from the clutches of dognappers. He continued his former life-style, roamed the streets at his pleasure but whenever Mr Sloboda's men approached – they could still be half a mile away – Victor rushed home at a speed which would put many a greyhound to shame.

When I was ten, my father died after a short illness. (Twenty years later he could have been saved, quite easily, with penicillin.) My family moved to Budapest and I was sent to school to Pécs, a neighbouring larger town. Victor was given away: a rich publican took him in. During the holidays I visited my grandmother at Siklós and I meant to visit Victor, too. But I was informed that he had been taken to the publican's farm in another village. I never saw Victor again but I know – or at least I was told – that he lived to a ripe old age. Perhaps he was happy at the publican's large farm; but perhaps he was mortally offended, and heartbroken. Perhaps he kept thinking, to his dying day, of his two loving chums and meditated on the unsteadiness and infidelity of the human race.

*   *   *

Horses, storks, swallows, geese, dogs – yes. But cats? We did have a cat, or cats – I am not even sure – and I do not remember any individual cat among them.

I remember occasions when cats gave birth to kittens. Some of the kittens were given away, a few were kept, but the majority of them were thrown by Auntie Kati into an outside loo to drown. I did not give a thought to these procedures. Today, when I recall them, I am horrified. But why? Is it my newly acquired English sensitivity? Here, too, they get rid of unwanted cats and kittens, the only difference being that here they 'put the dear little things to sleep' because they do not have old-fashioned peasant-style lavatories in which to drown them and are too cowardly to call a spade a spade. But I am not sure that the English procedure is quicker, less painful and more humane than Auntie Kati's cruder method.

While I was writing this chapter another suppressed memory forced itself upon me. Some of the boys of Siklós killed cats with bicycle pumps. They caught or stole cats and pumped water into their behinds. The cats swelled up to enormous, abnormal proportions and then burst, dying a horrifying and painful death. The boys were amused.

These events frightened me. I would not witness such a 'game' being played, the very idea of it made me sick. Yet somehow I was impressed by these tough boys, so much tougher than I; and their barbarous games put me off cats. This is a grave admission and it reflects one of the nastiest traits of human nature. 'What sort of animals are cats if they can be treated like this?' We have an innate tendency to admire the bully and look down upon his victim. I have heard people making contemptuous remarks about blacks because their grandfathers were slaves, as if this were *their* shame, not ours. Many people despise tramps and beggars but admire a man in a chauffeur-driven Rolls. The ultimate manifestation of this tendency occurred after the war when some people felt an impulse to recoil from the emaciated, subhuman, living skeletons liberated from the Nazi concentration and extermination camps, which they did not feel for the spick and span SS murderers. The story of the Siklós boys and the blown up cats all over again.

*   *   *

After I left Siklós, animals played no part in my life.

When I got to the secondary school in Budapest, called *gymnasium,* I suddenly found myself the shy, well-mannered, over-polite country bumpkin amid loud, shrewd, cynical and sophisticated metropolitan boys. I wanted to be like them, at all costs. I addressed everybody in the polite form of speech – using the equivalent of the French *vous* instead of the universally used *tu* – and it was only years later that I learned that I had created a craze. All the boys started calling one another *vous,* and mock courtesy became the fashion of the day. Country boys knew everything about animals, nature and so on; Budapest boys were utterly ignorant. So, in my keen endeavour to be like them, I – unconsciously but desperately – excluded all country matters from my mind. Once I created a roar of laughter in class when I was shown a large picture and failed – quite genuinely – to recognise a sparrow.

Animals did not figure in my life. In Budapest we had neither a dog, nor a cat. My next encounter with animals was years later, when I took my children to the Zoo. But the inhabitants of the Zoo are more exhibits than animals.

I was astonished by the English veneration of, and devotion to, the Cat. To me it was a curious perversity in a strange people to whom I took warmly but whom I failed really to understand. I made many references in books, articles and songs to this cult of the Cat. The English – I thought – had taken over cat worship from the ancient Egyptians and developed it further. Why do they adore *every* stray cat, I wondered, why don't they pick them on merit?

23

A man who had made fun of British cat-worship for several decades, I fell for Tsi-Tsa in the grand way – at first without even noticing it.

Half a Cat

*   *   *

'D'YOU think Tsi-Tsa is Jewish?' Eva asked me.

'She doesn't look Jewish,' I replied. 'But one never knows.'

'I hope she is.'

Eva is a passionate lover of the Jews. For a long time I didn't know what her religion was. I was not very much interested and whenever the subject came up and I asked a casual question she gave me an evasive answer. It was one of her friends who happened to mention that Eva was sad that she wasn't Jewish. She came from a Roman Catholic family from Czechoslovakia, and she resented the fact. Most of her friends were Jewish and so was her ex-husband. I think it was the delightful, wise and self-mocking Jewish humour that had gained her heart. She *hoped* that Tsi-Tsa was Jewish.

'Tsi-Tsa is Spanish,' I was able to report to her some time afterwards.

'Spanish or Catalan?' she asked. 'How do you know, anyway?'

'Spanish. I talked to that nice chap who keeps tinkering with his car outside the house.' (The man is Binky, a former sailor, now a drummer in the Talk of the Town and also a friend of mine.) 'He also knows

25

where Tsi-Tsa lives. In the next but one house in Fulham Road, on our left. He knows Tsi-Tsa's family. They're Spanish.'

This was sensational news, most unexpected.

'At least she is Mediterranean,' was Eva's verdict.

In the meantime Tsi-Tsa became a very regular visitor. When the door was opened she just walked in and made herself at home. When the door was closed she appeared on the patio, showed herself to us and miaowed until we opened the door for her. But soon she made herself independent and was able to come and go as she pleased.

To explain this I must say a few words about my house and its topography.

After a longish absence abroad, Eva and I came back to London in 1968 and had nowhere to live. I wanted to settle in Fulham because I love playing tennis and wanted to live near Hurlingham Club. After a brief search we found a flat which was near enough to the Club but it was in one of those prison-like blocks and we were not very enthusiastic about the idea of living there. Just before signing the contract – we had become resigned to the seemingly inevitable – Eva discovered an ad in the *Times* describing a charming little house in Fulham and we decided to have a look. We fell in love with the place and took it, with the idea of staying there for a few months. I have just completed the first decade in it. This seems to be a pattern in my life. In 1938 I came to England as a newspaper correspondent for a few weeks and have stayed here ever since; thirty years later I moved into a house for a couple of months and I doubt that I shall ever move out of it.

The story of the house, as I first heard it, was a delightful one. A well-known Harley Street specialist, who owns the neighbouring house in which Binky lives, and which faces onto Fulham Road, had it built for his spinster sister. By the time the house was ready, the sister was no spinster but had got married in Nottingham. That's how I, eventually, managed to get in. A romantic tale but – as is often the case with romantic tales – not true. It now appears that the Harley Street doctor has no sister, consequently she could not have got married and moved to Nottingham, or to any other town. But I resent reality spoiling nice stories. As far as I am concerned the house *was* built for the sister and she *did* get married in Nottingham and I hope her marriage was a great success and she has lived happily ever after even if she has never lived at all.

The house is small. You enter it through a neat little patio and then you step into a very large room – a drawing-room cum dining-room cum open-plan kitchen. This is the North Wing. The place is modern, the central heating is in the floor and Tsi-Tsa – as well as a number of other cats in Fulham, as we shall see later – soon discovered the delights of lying on the fitted carpet in winter-time. The South Wing contains one other room, the bedroom, as well as the bathroom and the loo. That's all, apart from two garages under the bedroom. In order to make room for the garages, the bedroom had to be raised: you have to climb seven steps from the North Wing to reach the South Wing. So the bedroom window is quite high up, it is really a first-floor window. Tsi-Tsa soon got into the habit of sitting in the window, watching humanity passing underneath, with the proverbial lofty disdain of cats. People sometimes stopped, talked to her, waved at her; mothers sometimes lifted their small children and instructed them: 'Say puss-puss to pussy.' Tsi-Tsa thought this damn silly and looked into the distance, completely ignoring mother and child. One day, to my great surprise, she left the house through the window. She got out, walked along the window-sill and after a huge and acrobatic leap landed on a brick wall below. She jumped off the wall – that was easy – and walked away. She always walked, she hardly ever ran. As a rule she walked slowly, like an ageing and careworn stockbroker.

She loved this way of departure and showed off with it. Sometimes she leaped out – when she knew she was being watched – and came back immediately. Occasionally she looked up at the window from the street, obviously contemplating the possibility of coming in the same way. But I knew this was impossible. Jumping down was difficult enough; leaping up was downright impossible. But I was wrong, Tsi-Tsa did not agree with me.

I was watching her when she made her first attempt – or at least her first successful attempt: she leaped up on the window-sill but there she got stuck. Before reaching the window she had to negotiate a very narrow part of the window-sill and there she was defeated. She fell off and although she got hold of something with her claws and did not fall right down, she was sufficiently frightened not to try again. What she did afterwards was leap up onto the window-sill, to show herself and miaow there, and when I opened the door, jump down and come in through the door. As my desk is under the window, I usually saw Tsi-Tsa appear on the window-sill, so she rarely had to wait long.

This became the routine for months. Then, one day, quite unexpectedly, Tsi-Tsa succeeded in negotiating that narrow bit on the window-sill and entered the house through the window. She was proud of her achievement and tried again. Soon she was able to perform that once perilous leap fifteen times a day without giving it a thought. Now she could come and go as she pleased, whether we were in or out. And she did. She was spending more and more time with us.

Other cats were watching Tsi-Tsa and tried to emulate her acrobatic feat, without success. But one night I came home and found three cats in the house. True, Tsi-Tsa was one of them but the two others were complete strangers: another black cat and a tabby. When I arrived the two strange cats panicked. It did not occur to them to try and leave through the window, where they had come in, and they started rushing around the house like mad. I opened the door for them and they stormed out. I panicked, too. If all the cats of Fulham can, after a little practice, do the trick, then I shall have to shut the window and keep Tsi-Tsa out, too. But no other cats came in for a long, long time and I never again saw my two night-time visitors.

*   *   *

'I should like to offer Tsi-Tsa something to eat,' I told Eva.

'She is very well looked-after. She often smells of perfume,' she replied.

'That's a typical female *non sequitur*,' I told her. 'What does her smell have to do with my wish to offer her food?'

'No – it is a perfect *sequitur* and yours is typical male insensitivity. She is beautifully looked after, consequently she is also well fed and isn't hungry.'

'But when we have visitors – human, not feline visitors – we offer them a cup of coffee or a drink, not because they are hungry or thirsty or because they stink, but in the way of ordinary, civilised hospitality. Tsi-Tsa must be deeply hurt that we are so horribly unhospitable to her. Don't you think?'

Eva did not reply. I bought some cat-food for Tsi-Tsa and offered it to her on a plate. On another plate I gave her milk. My hospitality was not refused. Indeed, Tsi-Tsa came even more frequently than before.

This was, of course, a fatal step. I did not know then that this is the way to steal a cat.

One day I was caught red-handed. In our little supermarket I had a tin of cat-food in my hand, when a nice-looking blonde lady came up to me, threw a glance at the object in my hand and asked me somewhat pointedly if I was the gentleman who lived in that little red-brick house round the corner. I admitted I was he.

'My cat keeps visiting you,' she said firmly.

'I know,' I replied. 'I started feeding her, not knowing that I was not supposed to do so. Too late now. She expects to be fed.'

The lady thought this over for a moment.

'That's all right,' she said kindly. 'We can share her.'

She added: 'This would have been a tragedy two years ago. I have a son who just adored that cat. But he is fourteen now and he has reached an age when he is more interested in girls than cats.'

'Perfect timing,' I nodded, 'as I have myself reached an age when I am more interested in cats than girls. May I ask you, Madam, are you Spanish?'

'No. I'm English. My name is May. The cat's name is Sooty.' She added: 'My husband is Spanish.'

So that was the key to the mystery.

'And is Tsi-Tsa . . . sorry, I mean Sooty, English or Spanish?'

31

She thought this over, perhaps for the first time.
'English. Sooty is English. Born and bred.'

'And – I hope you don't mind my asking: is she Jewish?'

This question needed another brief moment of careful thought.

'Yes. Definitely. She is Jewish. Sooty is an English Jewess.'

'By the way, you are sure that she is a *she*. A Jewess, not a Jew?'

'Of course I am sure. But don't be afraid, she won't have kittens. We had her neutered.'

So we shared Tsi-Tsa. I got half a cat. Friends started guessing which half belonged to me. The *Tsi* or the *Tsa*. There were ribald suggestions that it must be the *Tsa*.

(I have already described part of this scene in another book, *How to be Decadent,* but as it is an essential part of the story I must repeat it, with apologies to the few hundred thousand readers of that book.)

Soon afterwards, Eva got a lovely little cottage for herself in Knightsbridge and moved out, but she did not abandon me completely. She visited me now and then. So in the two wings of Dorncliffe Castle I led quite a pleasant life, with half a girlfriend and half a cat.

Saint Ginger and Others

*   *   *

ONE day – perhaps two years after the events described in the last chapter – I received a parcel of books from the United States. The books were not interesting but the string around the parcel was. When I was taking it off, Tsi-Tsa became terribly excited, leaping up to catch the end of it. She was a middle-aged cat now (nearly five) so she should have been more mature and dignified and less kittenishly playful. Friends suggested that this characteristic of hers was not genetic but purely environmental. I was the same type, they explained. I liked to play childish games, so she had been conditioned to fit in with my tastes. This is, of course, a completely untenable point of view. Tsi-Tsa would certainly have regarded chess for example, as a silly game, had I ever attempted to play *that* with her; but she found our string-game absorbing. The string, when not in use, hung on the door-handle of a cupboard near the Seven Steps, and she just sat down on the top step whenever she felt like playing and summoned me with a flick of her eyelid. This happened – at a rough estimate – about six times a day. We often played hide and seek, too (Tsi-Tsa hiding behind a curtain and showing her behind and wagging tail), but this was not half as popular as the string. Anyway, how unscientific can you get? How can anyone state that Tsi-Tsa's playfulness was environmental and not genetic without knowing her ancestors or at least her parents?

Of her ancestry and early life the world knew next to nothing. I often met May in Fulham Road and she – in instalments – told me as much as she herself knew. One day Tsi-Tsa, then still hardly more than a kitten, appeared on her doorstep and walked in to settle down – as she had walked in to me, a few years later.

May could add only two significant facts to this. Tsi-Tsa – she told me – had been taken to a vet and neutered: she had never known and could never know the joys of motherhood. The other fact was even more dramatic: still a kitten, she started wandering around and visiting people and, on one occasion, when she was crossing Fulham Road, she was knocked down by a car. She was badly hurt but May took her to a vet, looked after her and nursed her back to life. She fully recovered but never forgot the lesson and never again tried to cross Fulham Road.

*　　*　　*

One day May told me: 'You can have Sooty.'

'But I do have her.'

'You have only half. You can have the whole lot of her. She hardly ever comes to see us now.'

I had failed to realise that Tsi-Tsa, alias Sooty, was really living with me all the time. She slept on my bed or under it: sometimes I woke up and she was sleeping on my chest, with her right paw on my left shoulder,

34

embracing me in her own way. A uniquely original pose. She had all her meals – about eight a day – at my place. She came through the window a dozen times a day and sat on my lap when I was reading. She stayed there until the phone rang, then she jumped off. She came shopping with me. She accompanied me always to the same point, then sat down. When I reappeared ten minutes later, she emerged from under a car or jumped down from a wall and rejoined me on my way home.

Tsi-Tsa's moving in almost completely had little to do with my personal attractiveness. She used to be very happy in her other home, too. May lived in a second-floor flat and, in the early days, Tsi-Tsa could come and go there freely. Recently, however, a new tenant moved into the ground-floor flat and being very security-minded she kept the front-door locked all the time. Sometimes, when May thought she was at my place and I thought she was at hers, Tsi-Tsa was locked out. In the end Tsi-Tsa got fed up with this situation. Perhaps she was even offended and felt rejected. She is a very sensitive soul.

'But I shall always look after her when you are away,' May added, most generously.

I went away soon. She was as good as her word, she looked after Tsi-Tsa and all went well. But things started going wrong during my second absence, a few months later.

'She is not used to me any more,' May complained after my return. 'She may have forgotten us altogether. I used to come down at eleven at night, shout "Sooty!" and she answered my call. Now, on one occasion I had to search for her till two in the morning. Well, I'll still look after her when you're away, as I've promised, but it isn't so easy as I thought.'

It was soon after that that a series of disasters occurred to me, and even more to Tsi-Tsa, which prompted me to write this book.

* * *

And now to name-dropping. Before I relate our dramatic and traumatic experiences, I should like to say a few words about some remarkable cats I know.

The days when I thought that all cats were alike – that a cat was a cat was a cat – have long passed. I have become a great admirer of their sovereign ways, their independence, their incorruptibility, their insolence. They do want affection. They come for it when *they* need it, not when you condescend to give it. They like playing when *they* are in a playful mood, and not when *you* feel like dangling a piece of string. People sometimes accuse cats of being 'useless'. To whom? Why should cats be useful to humanity? What human-chauvinist-piggish attitude is this? Cats, by the way, have the same feline-chauvinist-piggish attitude to humanity but they are much more successful than we are. Cats find human beings useful domestic animals; we are permitted to feed them and, occasionally, to entertain them. Other people say that cats cannot be trained for anything. Cats do not see the point in jumping through hoops in a circus. They could jump, if they wanted to; they could jump better than dogs. But they jump when they feel like jumping and not when their turn comes, according to a programme printed without consultation with them.

By now I am fully aware that cats differ from one another as significantly – and are as much individuals – as humans, or more so. Some are straightforward, others devious; some are mean, others generous; some are callous, others gentle; some are tolerant, others quarrelsome; some are wild, others timid; some are rather silly while a few cats I know are brilliantly intelligent.

The first cat I got to know intimately, apart from Tsi-Tsa, was Harry. Actually, I am Harry's god-father. I bought him for Eva after she moved to her Knightsbridge cottage. She missed Tsi-Tsa, and she had always wanted a cat. When she looked ahead to her old age, she described herself as an old lady living in the country with her cat. Never with a man; never with a dog; never with a budgerigar: always with a cat. But her longing for Tsi-Tsa was not all that overwhelming and her old age was far ahead. She had other and more pressing reasons for acquiring a cat: she had found a mouse in her cottage. She told me that in the mornings, when she came down to her kitchen, she always found a mouse – the same one, she was sure – who took flight and scampered off in a panic. I asked her: what about a cat? But she wasn't sure. She rather liked the mouse. But she changed her mind when the mouse, instead of running away, started looking at her with an impertinent, 'Well, here I am – so what?' kind of expression on its face. Eva even spoke of a grin. It was its bad manners which brought disaster upon it. This has happened before and not only to mice. Crime can be forgiven; insolence never.

The Arab oil crisis was at its peak when I went to a

Fulham pet shop.
   'Have you got a cat for sale?' I asked.
   'No,' I was told.
   'No cats?'

The man shook his head: 'No cats.'

'Is there a shortage of cats?' I asked.

'A terrible shortage of cats.'

'Has this anything to do with the Arabs?' I asked suspiciously.

'Nothing to do with the Arabs.'

The man explained that at Easter time there was an abundance of cats but in November there was always a shortage of cats.

'I've got a cat, in fact,' he remarked, 'but he's not ready.'

'Not born yet?' I asked.

'He's born all right.'

I had no idea what he was talking about.

'Born but not ready?'

'That's it.'

'When will that cat be ready?'

'In two weeks' time.'

I returned to the shop in two weeks' time. The cat was there, born and ready. He was a tiny little ginger Tom, frightened to death. This must have been a horrible day for him. As he was deemed to be 'ready', he was taken from his mother and put in a cage in a pet-shop. Now he was being put into a brown box and taken away in that frightful prison. He miaowed desperately during the whole journey and made frantic efforts to break out. Eva fell in love with him at first sight. She still cannot forgive herself for leaving Harry alone on his first night in her house in that state. We were invited to the German Embassy and it would not have been easy to take Harry along.

The arrival of that tiny, miserable, frightened cat solved Eva's mouse problem for good. No mouse was ever seen again in her kitchen, grinning or serious. A small mouse, however, was discovered in the cottage opposite. Philip, the owner of that cottage, is a young barrister and not only a promising young lawyer but also a great man around the house. He can install central heating, make electrical repairs and mend his car. In other words he is a real wizard, greatly admired by me, a man whose mechanical skill ends at winding up my watch. Eva offered Philip to lend him Harry but Philip looked at the tiny cat and his pride was hurt. No, thanks. He had seen that infinitessimal mouse several times; he knew more or less where the hole was; it was ridiculous that he should not be able to catch it himself. He was crawling around on all fours for days. He saw the little mouse many times but it always got away with contemptuous ease. Having spent five full days crawling around on his knees, he gave up. Harry was called in. In came Harry, went behind the sofa and – fifteen seconds later – came out with the mouse between his teeth. Who said that barristers were cleverer than cats? Perhaps, in some ways; they are better at pleading. But in other, important, matters cats are cleverer than barristers.

Harry impressed me with other qualities, not just by being a better mouser than a young barrister. First, he became a real beauty, a miniature tiger. People in the mews remarked: 'An Errol Flynn among cats.' He was exceptionally intelligent, too. Most cats look at television and see nothing: they cannot discern shapes and forms. Once Harry and I were watching 'Match of the Day' together and for a full hour he chased the ball relentlessly. On another occasion, we were watching a nature programme and Harry chased all the birds. And he wanted to know how it works. He touched the screen with his paw; he looked behind the box; he touched the screen again; he shook his head. Harry loves television but not indiscriminately. Eva felt ill one day and was watching television in bed. Harry was sitting at her feet, watching, too. When 'Panorama' ended, a popular but vulgar comedy programme was announced. Harry yawned and walked off.

I have heard of another brilliant cat but I never had the honour of meeting her personally. She belonged to a lady who lived on her own and worked in an office. She left early in the morning and returned home after six in the evening. The lady's absence caused no difficulty because the cat had a flap door and could come and go as she pleased. The lady spoilt her cat – who doesn't? – but she was very strict on one single point. The cat received a tin of food in the morning, and no more until that was eaten up. If she let it go dry, as she often did . . . too bad. She had to eat the dry food before she got her more delicious supper. This was the only point of friction between the lady and her cat, but one day this too was solved. 'The triumph of patient education,' the lady thought on finding the cat's plate beautifully clean every evening. It took her months to discover what was really happening. The cat called in all the strays of the neighbourhood through the flap door and these poor cats were only too pleased to gobble up the rejects from the rich cat's plate.

If Harry is an Errol Flynn among cats, George is an Albert Einstein. George is a feline genius. He was named after me and I am proud to bear his name. He is of American origin. My son Martin met him in Boston when he was a kitten and brought him back to Lausanne, where he lives, although he already had two cats. One day George was naughty and Martin – not usually a strong disciplinarian – decided he ought to be punished. So he was put into the bathroom, with the door shut. Within half a minute George was out, and curled up on his favourite cushion. No one knew how he got out but next day the mystery was solved. This time it was the main door of the flat George opened, because he felt like a stroll outside. He jumped on the doorhandle, balanced himself on it until the door gave way and opened. When he wanted to return, he came back in the same way. Having discovered George's new habit, Martin locked the door for the night. But you cannot fob George off with such primitive tricks. He knows that it is the key that prevents him from opening the door and I saw him fiddling with the key. He cannot turn the key, of course, but he makes such an ungodly row by keeping on trying that Martin has to get out of bed and let him out. When he wishes to return at 5 a.m. he forces his way in, in the same way.

Last year – when George was already two and a half years old – he was naughty once again and had to be punished. This time Martin locked him in the kitchen. Half an hour later Martin thought that enough was enough and went to let George out. But there was no George in the kitchen. He was sunning himself on the balcony, outside the kitchen.

It takes quite a cat to observe how a door is opened and even to try turning a key. But one would think that other cats – while unable to invent these methods themselves – would be able to imitate them. But Martin's two other cats never even try to imitate George. They simply wait for George and rely on him to let them in or out. I maintain that the other cats are too dumb even to copy George; Martin begs to differ. He says they are even more intelligent than George, and exploit his cleverness. They let George do the dirty work.

*　　*　　*

A friend of mine once remarked that she had never noticed prams in the streets until she herself became pregnant; then she realised that the streets were full of them. Similarly, in the pre-Tsi-Tsa days I but rarely noticed cats. Today I know all the cats of Fulham, strays as well as prosperous local burghers. Most are only nodding aquaintances; a few are intimate friends.

The greatest character and the nicest of them all is Ginger. He turned up about three years ago and started visiting me. Once again, I did not know what he was called so I had to give him a generic name, as I had given Tsi-Tsa once upon a time. When Ginger first appeared on the scene, he looked awful. He was thin, his fur was filthy and dishevelled and there was a gaping wound on his back. There was something pathetic in his helplessness and something appealing in his demeanour. I fed him occasionally. He was always hungry and his appetite was voracious. He was fed on the patio but soon discovered that there was nearly always food on Tsi-Tsa's plate. So he sneaked or rushed in whenever the opportunity arose. The postman rang; a visitor arrived; I went out for a

43

moment to the dustbin or to water the flowers outside. As soon as the door opened, Ginger jumped down from the wall like a tiger, rushed in and raided Tsi-Tsa's plate. Tsi-Tsa was madly jealous. She attacked Ginger and slapped his face with her paws. Ginger never resisted or retaliated. He just retreated a few steps. When Tsi-Tsa's fury was spent, Ginger moved forward with measured steps, slowly and sadly, and gobbled up whatever food he found on the plates.

(Very well, I thought proudly, better that Tsi-Tsa be a donor than a beggar. Then I discovered that my immediate neighbour, Binky, had a very old, black cat who hardly ever left the house. I asked Binky if he, too, was on Tsi-Tsa's visiting list. 'She sometimes rushes in, when the door is open,' said Binky, 'eats up my cat's food and rushes out.')

Then things got sorted out. A girl in one of the neighbouring houses took Ginger in. Now he had a home. His appearance improved, his fur became smooth if not exactly silky, but his wound healed only very, very slowly. For some reason he kept to his habit of coming to me for breakfast. He arrived at 8.30 or so and knocked on the door with his paws. When I opened the door, he rushed in to pinch a piece of fish from Tsi-Tsa, received a slap or two from her which he did not seem to mind, then followed me when he saw me carry his own food out to the patio. Whenever I came home late at night, Ginger recognised my car and came up to greet me. He wanted to be stroked; he wanted a little affection; and he always wanted food. He was so hungry all the time that people began to say that he had tape-worms. But he had no worms, only an insatiable appetite. And yet he was always ready to share his food with the poor. Or just with friends and relations. If George was the cleverest cat, Ginger was the most generous. Sometimes a black and white cat was invited for breakfast (Ginger's son, they said) and occasionally a large, bushy tailed ginger cat, too (his sister-in-law, I was told). Ginger always shared his food with them and offered them old-fashioned, almost oriental hospitality.

When Beelzebub turned up, Ginger rose to real greatness. Beelzebub was a tiny, frightened, stray kitten, half ginger, half black – certainly most peculiar, with a small, vicious, devilish face. He was very wild and trusted no one. He was poorer and much hungrier than Ginger and Ginger immediately took him under his wing, if this be the right metaphor for a cat. The two cats walked together, hunted together, crossed the streets together and came for breakfast together. Ginger not only tolerated Beelzebub, but having eaten a little, he walked away and left the rest to him. Later, as we shall see, Ginger showed the same touching gentleness to his arch-enemy, Tsi-Tsa, when she needed it. If there are saints among cats Ginger should be canonised.

Then Ginger started turning up for breakfast alone once again. I looked for Beelzebub but he seemed to have disappeared.

Soon afterwards I paid one of my rare visits to the Hungarian Section of the BBC, where I had worked during the war. A former colleague told me that he had just quoted a remark from one of my books. I asked which remark.

'You said that humanity consists of three kinds of people. Those who have worked for the BBC, those who are working for the BBC and those who will work for the BBC. And you said that those who are out, all try to get in and those who are in, all try to get out.'

Yes, I remembered that from one of my early books and being not less vain than the next man, was pleased that he remembered it too.

I came home and met the lady from the house opposite who knew all the cats around. She took a kindly interest in Beelzebub (whom she called Jemima), fed her, too, and tried to tame her. I asked her if she knew what had happened to Beelzebub.

'Oh, Jemima,' she said, 'She joined the BBC.'

'In what capacity?'

'There was a lady in the house and she said that the BBC needed a cat and she took her. She loved Jemima so she'll be all right.'

'The BBC is huge,' said I. 'Do you know which department she joined?'

'All I know is that she has joined the BBC.'

I was sorry to have lost a little friend; but pleased to have been vindicated as a prophet.

A Year of Disasters

*   *   *

NOW followed a year of disasters. I must not give the impression that I spent all of it in deep gloom, or that I was unhappy. For that I would need more than a few accidents, burglaries, fires etc. But I did not really *enjoy* any of these events. They affected both of us – Tsi-Tsa and me – in various ways. We did not always see eye to eye on them. Tsi-Tsa, for example, was definitely amused by the burglaries; she thought them funny. Our sense of humour is different; we seem to laugh at different things. But then we came to the last two disasters in the series, and they affected both of us equally.

The first disaster I have already described else-where.* It all began with a tennis elbow which started bothering me at the end of May. It was not really painful and as I was to go away at the beginning of June for some weeks, I did not pay too much attention to it. When I returned to London at the end of July – not having played tennis for two months – I had nearly forgotten about it. Alas, it had not forgotten about me. I started playing a lot – three

*In the *Sunday Times,* on the 24th July, 1977, in a piece entitled 'How to be a Tennis Casualty'. The following is a slightly changed version of that piece.

hours on the first day – and my tennis elbow returned with a vengeance.

I went to see Mr S, a Persian physiotherapist who had successfully cured me of the same disability seven years before. Then I asked a doctor friend of mine whether I should consult a physician or a physiotherapist. 'A physiotherapist any day,' she advised me firmly. I was surprised and she explained: 'Tennis elbow is not a serious enough illness for good doctors to give a lifetime of research to it.'

'I see,' I nodded.

'A further difficulty is,' my doctor friend continued, 'that people do not die of tennis elbow so we have no proper *post mortem* reports either.'

'I am sorry,' I said and felt a little embarrassed at not having died of tennis elbow.

'So a physiotherapist is the answer. A man who dedicates his life to curing tennis elbow will know more about it than any doctor.'

Mr. S is a fully trained physiotherapist who does diverse jobs at a hospital, lives outside Queen's Club, and is a keen tennis player himself. Most of his private practice consists of curing his ailing tennis partners and their friends. Last time I always had my treatment in the company of Arthur Ashe and Charles Pasarell and Mr S's surgery was the only place under the sun where our tennis-game could bring Ashe and me together. My tennis elbow was cured in about six weeks.

On this occasion once again he told me not to play tennis. I feigned surprise and asked him – as all tennis maniacs do – if I could play *a little*.

'With that arm? No, you can't play with that arm at all,' he replied firmly.

With that arm was the operative phrase. All right. What about the other arm? After all, I have two. Next day I was out at Hurlingham Club, practising against the wall with my left hand. For an ordinary, right-handed person this sounds nonsense; how can anyone even hit a ball with his left hand unless he is left-handed? I have often thought that I would have become left-handed if they had let me. But in my youth such perversity as writing or playing tennis with one's left hand was absolutely out of the question (even slightly immoral, I believe), so I was forced to use my right hand.

Some people called me – somewhat flatteringly – ambidextrous. But as a result of my right-handed education – although I do everything with my left hand unless I was definitely taught not to – I am rather clumsy with both hands. 'He has two left hands' we used to say about clumsy people in Hungary and indeed, *ambi-sinistral* would be a more fitting description of my skills. On this occasion I developed a reasonable left-handed forehand in no time.

A few days later I felt strong enough to challenge an old friend for a game. She is a nice girl but no great hand at tennis, just the opponent I needed. We played a set and although normally I am not too keen on winning – I'd rather lose a good game than win a bad one – on this occasion I was inordinately pleased with myself when I succeeded in beating her. We started a second set and during that set I hit a ball which I shall remember for the rest of my life. A soft, nice, highly-bouncing ball came to my right hand side and I attempted a strong, effective, left-handed back-hand-return. But I hit the ball into my right eye, with full force.

The blow made me dizzy for a minute. Then I looked around and was surprised to realise that I could see. So I continued playing. This was a foolish thing to do for a number of reasons; one – and not the most important one – was that I could not really focus on the ball, and failed to see it properly and lost the second set in no time.

Later I went to see my doctor. I told him what happened. He took out an ophthalmoscope – one of those telescopic things with strong lights inside – examined my eye and told me that the ball had done no damage to it. Before letting me go, however, he led me to the chart and told me to read it. The result was disheartening. Although I had not noticed that my eyesight was worse than before, I could read only the three huge letters on top. Everything else looked like a black mass. In that case, my doctor said, off I must go to an eye-hospital and the sooner the better. In other words: immediately. As it was Friday afternoon, he sent me to the one eye-hospital in the West End which has a 24-hour service.

I went to the Casualty Department and was seen by a pretty and charming young lady who looked fourteen but must have been more. She looked into my eyes with the help of various, impressive and huge instruments and saw nothing and said nothing. She looked again and she told me: 'We'll have to put some drops into your eyes.'

Naïve girlie, I thought. Innocent maiden. Little do you know what that means. I am a peaceful, law-abiding citizen until someone tries to touch my eyes. Some years ago something fell into my eye in New York. It hurt more and more, so in the end I went into a drugstore and asked the chemist if he knew a doctor. I needed no doctor, he said, he would take it out for me. He told me to sit down and meant to turn up my eyelid. As soon as he touched me, I boxed him in the stomach with such force that he fell against the counter.

'I'm sorry,' said I.

'That's perfectly all right,' he replied with sus-
picious courtesy. He waved to two thuggish-looking
gentlemen – they must have been gangsters in private
life – who came forward with the slow, languid
movements of the guys who used to partner Edward
G. Robinson. They pushed me down, each of them
gripping one of my arms and one of my legs. They had
grips of steel, I could not move at all although I tried
desperately to kick the man again. He worked with
sadistic pleasure, took a speck of dust out of my eye,
bathed it and soothed it and when he finished,
motioned the two hired killers that they might let me
off. I asked him how much I owed him. He said:
nothing. I insisted. But to no avail. He said it was his
pleasure to help a visitor in distress. Now I
remembered the New York drugstore-man and really
forced myself to be as co-operative as I could. As a
result two nurses – one Chinese, the other West
Indian – after about twenty minutes of struggle
succeeded in putting half the amount of the required
drops into my eyes but, at least, there was no violence.

Twenty minutes later (it takes some time for the
stuff to work) that charming child looked into my eyes
again. She could see nothing and looked at me – I
thought – reproachfully. I was not playing the game,
she seemed to imply. This was Casualty Department
and I had come with something unusual. She looked
and looked and saw nothing. Perhaps a few drops in
her eyes might help, I thought.

She left the room and returned with a young Indian
(or Pakistani) doctor. He must have been on his way
home when caught. He looked into my eyes and saw
nothing, but as I still could not read even the large

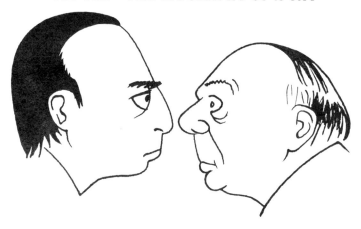

letters, something, patently, must have been wrong. He took me to his surgery, made me lie on a couch, examined me with larger and larger and brighter and brighter ophthalmoscopes and took me back to the young lady. On the way back he gave me a few words of consolation.

'There is no danger of your losing your eyes immediately,' he said. That cheered me up no end.

Then he explained to the young lady – as if I were not present and as if all patients were too stupid, in any case, to understand a diagnosis containing a Latin word or two – that the ball had nothing to do with my troubles. In fact, the ball was a blessing in disguise because it had made me come to the hospital. The truth was that some arteries in my eyes were hardening. If there was some fluid in my eyes, then although they would make an effort to treat them, the result would be very doubtful and I might go blind in a short time. If there was no fluid, then my eyes would last another year or two, but in that latter case there was absolutely nothing they could do. I watched the young (he was about thirty) Indian and gained two main impressions.

First, that he wanted to impress the young woman. 'You could diagnose nothing in half an hour and I, in a few minutes, can assess a very complex situation. Aren't I wonderful?' My second feeling was that he rather enjoyed giving me this gloomy forecast. Perhaps it was just the not unusual sadism of medical men mixed with a tiny racial element. He was perfectly courteous and instructed me to make an appointment for next Tuesday, i.e. four days later, when a proper diagnosis would be made. Well, I wondered, if there was no proper diagnosis as yet, wasn't it just a trifle hasty to indicate that I was going blind in two years if I was lucky and sooner if I was not so lucky?

Saying goodbye to the young lady, I asked her, too, how bad my eyes were. She told me – very nicely – that after a certain age one must expect things to go slightly wrong.

Next Tuesday I appeared at the eye hospital as instructed and was examined, once again, by the young Indian registrar. He put another pint of those loathsome drops into my eyes and we went through Friday's routine once again. Then he told me: 'You need fluorescein angiography.'

Some people do not know what fluorescein angiography is and I belonged to that happy group. But if I needed it, I needed it. The doctor explained that this was extremely urgent. If I made an official appointment at reception, they would give me a date two months' ahead.

I meant to interrupt and ask him how long it took to get an appointment in a case of no extreme urgency. If I came back at four o'clock – he said kindly – he would do the examination straight away. Could I make it? I said that of course I would make myself free. He also explained that fluorescein angiography was essentially photography of the eye. They would give me an injection but otherwise it was simple, harmless photography.

At lunch-time I pondered over this injection business. If it is a trifle difficult to lift my eyelids, it is downright impossible to give me an injection. I could not recall the time when anyone succeeded in giving me one. But I clearly recalled the day my sister – a doctor herself, in New York – chased me with a syringe with the piston pulled out while I, with a fever of 102, hid in a cupboard. I was about fifty-four at that time. My sister only wanted to give me an ordinary, common-or-garden injection. This doctor obviously wanted to give me an injection into the eye. I had heard about these injections into one's eye and I was terrified. I also knew that he would not be able to do it without putting me to sleep.

At four o'clock I duly appeared at the hospital. They poured another bucketful of drops into my eyes. There was a slight struggle. After a while the young Indian doctor took me down to the basement and started taking photographs of my eyes. Twenty minutes later another doctor and a nurse appeared.

She took a syringe and told me to take my jacket off and roll up my shirtsleeve. So I would not get the injection into my eye. In fact, I got an intravenous injection into my left arm and they kept the needle in for about two minutes while they were taking further pictures – one every three seconds. No man had succeeded in giving me an intravenous injection before; indeed, few had been so foolish as to try; but this time I was so relieved and delighted that the injection did not go into my eye that I behaved like a little lamb and when it was all over I offered my right arm.

They did not take it. They had injected some dye into my veins which turned me quite yellow for a while and made me pee beautiful golden stuff for two days. Then I was told to come back in four weeks' time, on October 1, when they would give me their final diagnosis. In the meantime it seemed that there was no fluid on my eyes and that was a very good thing. Yes, I remembered that it meant that I had about two years before going blind.

Another doctor friend – hearing all this – remarked that it was scandalous to wait with such results four weeks.

'It takes a few minutes to develop the pictures,' he commented.

*　　*　　*

Everybody has discussed with friends what it would be like going blind. Some people indulge in heated arguments to decide whether it is better to be completely blind or stone deaf – as if anybody ever had the choice.

When you are told by specialists in a hospital that you, actually, are going blind the whole thing ceases to be a parlour game.

How did I react?

First of all, I debated whether I should kill myself. I am not the suicidal type. Never in my life did I contemplate suicide seriously – or indeed, non-seriously. This time I considered it coolly and – I can honestly claim – without a touch of self-pity. After all, I am over sixty, I thought I was in reasonably good shape until I heard abou the state of my eyes. I have had a good life; I have enjoyed every minute of it; I have lived well; I have two nice children and some good friends, very near to my heart; I have had some so-called successes – in other words I have had a fair run. Was it not better to pack up before I became a burden to anyone – a particularly hateful notion. But my considerations were not all as altruistic as that. Up to now, I thought, I have lived well; who the hell wants to start vegetating so late in life?

Eva often asked me what I wanted to do in real old age. I told her that I would try to get into an old men's home – I had my eye on a lovely place in Fulham, on the river – and I wanted to read a lot; and not only read but especially *re-read,* one of the great joys when it comes to truly great books.

I especially hoped to re-read Thomas Mann's Joseph tetralogy, *War and Peace* and Proust. I told Eva that I might keep – secretly – my membership in Hurlingham and slip over for a set or two, occasionally. She shook her head in disapproval.

'You say this as a joke. The trouble is that you mean it; the still greater trouble is that you would be perfectly happy.'

She was right, of course. I foresaw some dangers to my plan. I might not be able to get into that Old

Men's Home; or my service might deteriorate
abominably after eighty-five and no one would want
to play with me. But never in my life had it occurred to
me, not even in my worst dreams, that I might not be
able to *read*. This I found quite unbearable, so I
thought a quiet act of suicide, without drama or fuss,
would be a reasonable solution.

But I couldn't do it to Tsi-Tsa. The world would
go on exactly as before. I would be the subject of
animated conversation at a few places for a few days
and then I would be forgotten. But Tsi-Tsa's whole
life would change. No, I couldn't do it to Tsi-Tsa, she
would never forgive me. Yet, I hesitated.

Then I happened to listen to a radio programme
and afterwards I felt a little ashamed. A twenty-
seven-year-old army officer who had served in
Northern Ireland had a bomb explode in his face and
was blinded in both eyes. He told the interviewer that
he had never seen his little daughter who was born
after the accident. But he could *feel her,* he said, and
that brought her very near to him. He described how
he had adjusted his life to the new circumstances.
When his little daughter was mentioned again, he
broke down and cried.

'Sometimes it *is* a little difficult,' he explained.

If a young man can take it so bravely, how can I be
such a coward? He has to face a whole long life; how
can I shirk a few years, just because sometimes it *will*
be a little difficult.

Suddenly I saw certain aspects of my life from
completely new angles. How nice that I have a very
small house. I had often complained that I needed at
least one extra room – how lucky that I did not have

it! I had never rejoiced that my house was all on the ground floor, but that was just what the doctor would order! Well, the eye-specialist. What a pity that I was not addicted to music. But one could learn, and train oneself.

I tied something over my eyes and made experiments to find out how I could move around. It was not difficult to reach any part of the house, except that objects on the floor – a heater here, a small coffee table there – got in the way and I tumbled over them. In bed I tried to put the light off – just to pull a string – without looking. I had done it hundreds of times, without giving a thought to this feat. Now that I meant to do it I could not manage. I just could not find that dangling string. A good thing, I thought, that I would not have to put the light on or off in the future.

I also tried typing. I have been using typewriters all my life. I knew how to type before I could write, at the age of four. This stands to reason; it is easier to push down keys than form letters. So, no doubt, blind typing would be child's play. My experiment proved an utter failure. I always hit nearby keys but the text was quite unreadable.

If the knowledge that you will be hanged in the morning concentrates the mind wonderfully, the knowledge that you will go blind soon does almost as good a job. Let me explain here something which looks like a non sequitur but isn't – that I have never been worried about my age, except once, when I turned forty. Forty is a dreadful age, or at least, it was for me; then I realised for the first time that I would not live forever. This rather upset me for two or three days and I had profound thoughts about eternity, the futility of existence and the general idea of perishing. Then I shrugged my shoulders and accepted the situation. Well, if that's the way it is, I thought, let it be.

But even in my profoundest thoughts about my fate, I realised no more than that one day I would *die*. The thought simply never occurred to me that I would not lead a healthy and active life until I breathed my last; that I would not be able to play tennis, to write my books and chase women, whatever the end-result of such chases might be. The possibility of going blind had never crossed my mind. It is true that I rarely thought of illness and disaster. I had not seen a doctor for years. I never went for check-ups because I believed that if you start being preoccupied with diseases you will catch them. Similarly, I had always refused to buy a first-aid kit.

My tennis partner, after the accident with my eye, had told me to go home and bathe it with something or other. I said that I did not have the stuff. She said that every first-aid kit contains it. I replied that that was quite possible but I did not have a first-aid kit. She refused to believe me and made me promise that I would buy one next day. I refused to promise, I had never had a first-aid kit and would not buy one now. But wasn't I stubborn and stupid, she asked. Possibly, I answered, but once you start buying first-aid kits you start having accidents. You run after your money; you tend to turn it into a good investment.

Besides I have hated amateurs all my life. If you have an accident, call a doctor. I have never taken a sleeping pill and my medical chest contains a bottle of aspirins and nothing else. Sometimes I run out of aspirins, too. But now, as at the age of sixty plus, I suddenly realised that I might not only be dead one day but much worse: I might be ill, a cripple and

blind. I thought of some young lady friends who, astonishingly, liked me. I thought I ought to terminate all such contacts. It is one thing to spend some time with an old man; quite another to spend it with a blind old man. That was the saddest thought of all.

I considered my financial situation. With my royalties (hoping for the best), with Public Lending Rights (hoping for something better than the best) and with the then not too distant old-age pensions (State and private) I should be able to manage. Besides, I should be able to make some money even if blindness slowed me down. Reading might be a little difficult, I pondered. On the other hand, my expenses would be substantially reduced. I would not be able to travel much; I should have to give up my car which ought to save me quite a bit. It's cheap to be blind, I realised with some relief. Perhaps, I added, it is cheaper still to be dead.

Here I paused. Am I taking this impending disaster sufficiently seriously? Or am I joking about it? And if I am – why? Is it my lack of imagination, not really being able fully to realise its horror, or is it my inborn inability to take *anything* seriously? Is it courage or cowardice? Am I trying to tame this disaster, not daring to look it in the face, trying to be chummy with Blindness and trying to convince Blindness that we are friends, both on the same side of the fence, so that it cannot be really ghastly to me?

It was, of course, a mixture of these attitudes. I could not surrender to doom. Someone asked me (you do get these questions) whether I would be able to go on playing tennis? 'Oh yes,' said I, 'with a white racket.' What was I doing, for goodness sake? Turning the greatest tragedy of my life into a joke? Yes. That's what I have always done. With varying success.

The reaction of my friends varied. I did not go around discussing my troubles, but quite a few of them knew about them and, naturally, I was grateful for genuine interest. Some were visibly shaken and told me too loudly, too jovially that this was nonsense, I would not lose my sight. Others tried to joke it away – just as I did. One person remarked: 'You are lucky. To have such a long notice. You can get prepared.'

'But I am rather used to my eyes,' I told him. 'I shall miss them however long the notice.'

Then the idea cropped up that I ought to have a second opinion. I agreed but said I ought to wait till October 1, when I would get the hospital's diagnosis. 'Why?' friends asked. 'Well, I want a second opinion. If I go before that, I'll get a first opinion.' This sounded very convincing to all except to my woman-doctor friend (whose views on physicians and physiotherapists I have quoted) and she said that I was talking rot and should go to see a specialist without delay.

So I went. Mr H is an eminent eye-surgeon in Harley Street and also consultant at one of our great hospitals. He inspired immediate confidence. He started examining me and, at an early stage, I noticed, he lost all interest in my left, undamaged eye. He poured drops into the right eye only. After a thorough examination he said: 'It was the tennis ball that damaged your eye. I have no doubt about this whatsoever. The ball has damaged the retina. The retina, however, has a wonderful self-healing capacity and yours seems to be healing. Avoid all violent exercises: diving, water-skiing, wrestling and – above all – tennis. Come back in a month's time.'

I asked him whether this meant that even in the worst case, if I was to lose my right eye, I would still keep the left one. Yes, it meant that.

It all depends in which direction you are travelling. Had anyone told me a few weeks before that I was to lose an eye, I would not have cherished the thought; but now I was one of the happiest men in town. My brother had reminded me a few days before in a letter, sent from New York where he lives, that when we were both very young I had told him that one should take care of one's penis because one had only one; eyes were less important because one had two of them. A remarkable proof of sagacity in a man of nineteen.

* * *

I had every intention of keeping my appointment at the eye hospital on October 1. I thought it was elementary courtesy; also – having been told that I would go blind in both eyes – I wanted to hear now what their diagnosis was.

On September 21 I received a letter from the hospital's Medical Secretary (written on the previous day) inviting me to the Casualty Department for – believe it or not – fluorescein angiography on October 8. In the accompanying leaflet I was warned: 'In some patients this investigation is *extremely urgent*.' (My italics.) There was not a single word about the fact that I was supposed to get the *result* of this extemely urgent examination on October 1. Not a word that something had gone wrong and the examination had to be repeated. Not a word that they were aware that the examination had, in fact, been carried out at all. I wrote back saying that I had had a second opinion, I knew now what was wrong with my eyes and I did not wish to waste their time. Mr H the specialist, told me subsequently that he fully agreed: 'I don't think that line of investigation would serve any useful purpose in your case.'

But I could not help wondering about that eye-hospital, supposedly one of the best in the country. They first saw me in August. I would presumably have had the result of the October 8 examination on November 8 in an 'extremely urgent' case. What would have happened between August and November if their original diagnosis had been right? After all, not *all* their diagnoses can be wrong. What about those people who do not or cannot go to a Harley Street specialist? Do we have quite a few blind men tapping around the streets with white sticks just because 'you know what the Health Service is like?'

*   *   *

In the meantime my tennis elbow was healing beautifully.

'A good thing you didn't play at all,' Mr S told me. 'Most people are too weak to stop altogether and go on playing. That's disastrous. You were really lucky that your eyes prevented you from playing.'

Well, we all have to be lucky some time.

Now, months later, my eye has completely healed. I can play tennis again. And my tennis elbow is slowly coming back.

*   *   *

That was the situation when I first wrote about my eyes. Alas, I was much too optimistic. My eyes *are* deteriorating, but not too fast. I can still read (with a magnifying glass) and I can still play tennis (without a magnifying glass). But I see the ball too late and my game which, once upon a time, I could proudly call mediocre, has now become rather poor.

I may not go blind, after all; or I may. No one knows. I would not like it at all. One is selfish and one thinks, first of all, of oneself. But if I went blind it would be quite awful for Tsi-Tsa, too. I might have to buy a dog and that would ruin her life. How could she possibly tolerate a dog when in her fierce jealousy she refuses to accept even Ginger? Perhaps, after all, it would have been fairer to Tsi-Tsa if I had committed suicide.

*   *   *

Tsi-Tsa was more involved in Disaster Number Two. I am not suggesting that she actually committed the burglary or was an accomplice. I have never had any reason to doubt her integrity. But her behaviour was somewhat off-putting.

When I came home that evening at about 9.30, the first extremely unusual phenomenon that caught my attention was that Tsi-Tsa and Ginger were sitting, most amicably, side by side, on the pavement in front of the house. They both wore stupefied yet amused

expressions on their faces. Later I realised that these expressions declared: 'Well, I have always known that human beings are foolish and often behave incomprehensibly. But what the hell was *this* in aid of?'

I found the large sliding door, leading in from the patio, forced open and the house in a frightful mess: drawers pulled out and emptied on the floor, clothes and the contents of other cupboards forming various heaps on the carpet, some glasses broken, pieces of furniture upset. The two cats simply loved it. They could sit on piles of files or heaps of garments, and could explore all the objects lying around. Their enjoyment was enormous and obvious. There was one thing I enjoyed, too. My television set, record-player, camera, and recording-machine were all near the door, ready to be taken away, but had been left behind. I must have disturbed the burglars with my early return home. They departed with a very modest loot (my pocket calculator, all my drinks and a few other small objects). I phoned the police and soon a small boy arrived. He looked quite sweet in police uniform. When I was a child, we were often dressed in naval uniform; perhaps police uniform was the new fashion. He was, I thought, a trainee to be a trainee.

'Look at this mess,' I told him. 'Is this worse than usual or is it just normal?'

'I don't know. This is the first time I've ever seen a burglary.'

I asked him to go home, it was past his bedtime. His mother must be getting worried. Next morning the CID came and told me that there were an awful lot of burglaries nowadays. He also declared that burglaries were an awful nuisance. He seemed to disapprove of them. He also thought that if people were honest and absolutely upright there would be fewer burglaries. I nodded and as I was determined to contribute something to this fascinating conversation, remarked that if, on the other hand, people were even more dishonest there would be more. He thought this over, drank another whisky and replied thoughtfully: 'Perhaps . . .' (With three dots. I could distinctly hear the three dots in his voice.) We spent about an hour and a half in this agreeable chat, then he jumped up and told me that he had to rush away as he had to visit several more burglary victims. Half an hour later the finger-print expert arrived, went through the whole house for finger-prints, found none but explained to me that I was not to worry because it did not make the slightest difference.

The criminal investigation thus concluded, I spent two days in tidying up. A month or so later the burglars visited me again and took everything they had left behind on the first occasion and made an even bigger mess. The whole show was repeated, complete with CID men and finger-print expert, except that this time the policeman who came right after my telephone call was so old that I had to help him into a chair. I was an experienced victim by now and knew the routine. I told the CID man that I sympathised with the police to some extent but wondered why they were wasting their time with such empty formalities. Perhaps they could catch more burglars if they investigated less. My suggestion for reform was received coolly.

'It's not what they steal,' a friend, herself the victim of several burglaries, said 'but the fact that they enter your house. I resent the loss less than the intrusion.'

I replied that I resented the loss more than the intrusion but as the two went together I thought the discussion was somewhat academic.

The burglaries interfered with Tsi-Tsa's everyday life. I dared not leave the window slightly open (although they were fixed and could not be opened further from the outside) and this interfered with her free movements. I had to install a burglar-alarm and was told that a set of keys (four altogether) had to be left with a neighbour. I gave the keys to Binky, and I did not have another set left for May to come in to feed Tsi-Tsa when I was away. This small change, as we shall see, had a tremendous effect on Tsi-Tsa's life. And on mine.

'That ball in your eye plus the two burglaries make up the series of three disasters,' quite a few friends reassured me. 'It's all over now. From now on all will be well.'

When my car exploded (with me in it) and burnt out completely, it was explained to me that the *two* burglaries ought to have been counted as *one* disaster so the series of three has only now been completed.

The worst disaster of all however, followed after all these. But perhaps it belonged to a new series.

The Lady Vanishes

*   *   *

BINKY sounded hesitant and upset.

'I don't know.'

'You don't know where Tsi-Tsa is?'

'I don't. She's disappeared.'

'Disappeared?'

'You left on a Friday. After the following Tuesday no one saw her. She's gone. I've looked everywhere. I've asked everybody. No sign of her.'

I put the receiver down. The date of this conversation was Sunday, June 5, 1977. I arrived home on that day at 5.45; I phoned Binky two minutes later.

*   *   *

On May 13 (a Friday; quite a few people pointed out that if I started journeys on a Friday the 13th, I was asking for it) I left for a PEN Club Conference in Hamburg, then drove on to Switzerland, back to Germany, on to Austria and finally home.

During my trip I heard in Munich that a very good friend of mine B, the actor, had died in Budapest. He had played quite a part in my life. We shared a flat in London in 1939 and 1940, sometimes starving and sometimes living lavishly, chasing women all the time and selling a play to Selznick, through the services

72

and help of Noël Coward. I wrote the play, B was to play the leading part in it. But war broke out and as I refused to go on with him to the United States (although we had our visas stamped into our passports) he returned to Hungary. He went through a tough time during the war but became the leading actor of his country, a kind of Hungarian Laurence Olivier. He had settled down with a charming wife and two children he loved. He was a happy man. Now he had died of cancer of the lung.

B was dead and now Tsi-Tsa had disappeared. I have already mentioned that I had no extra set of keys for May who, as a rule, looked after Tsi-Tsa when I was away. It was Binky who had the keys and when the burglar-alarm was installed he was registered with the police as the key-holder. It would have been complicated to change this and then change back after a fortnight. In any case, May had told me that Tsi-Tsa hardly knew her any more. Tsi-Tsa knew Binky very well.

After two burglaries my main preoccupation was to make the house safe against burglars during my absence. It was a reassuring thought that Binky would come in twice a day. He could watch my front door from his flat. It did not occur to me to worry about Tsi-Tsa. I knew that she would be annoyed and a little unhappy about being left alone but I also knew that she would still be better off than in a kennel. Cats are territorial animals – I told myself – and as long as they are in their normal surroundings and are being fed, they are all right.

I was not too upset on hearing the news of Tsi-Tsa's disappearance. I am a delayed-action man.

When something unexpected or dreadful happens (such as an explosion when I am sitting in my car) I remain as cool as a cucumber. When I hear some very bad news, I nod. It takes time to sink in. A few hours later I start to feel deadly tired, my limbs become leaden. And then, slowly, I start reacting emotionally – although hardly ever too emotionally.

What could have happened to Tsi-Tsa? Run over? Surely, then someone would have seen it or found the body. Taken away? Stolen? Possibly. I had heard of

gangs who go around stealing cats for their fur. Tsi-Tsa's black fur was shiny and exceptionally beautiful, I thought – rather proudly. Or did she die of a heart attack? But again, someone would have found her body and told me about it. Tsi-Tsa was a well known character in these parts of Fulham.

Black Tuesday, Binky mentioned, was May 17, i.e. nearly three weeks had passed between her disappearance and my return. A long time. This was no temporary absence, a cat spending a night out or sleeping away for a night or two. One could not shrug it off by remarking 'Well, she will turn up'. She had been given plenty of time for turning up. I had to face it: it seemed more likely than not that Tsi-Tsa was dead.

The reaction was late to set in. I went out to dinner and spent the evening quite happily, drinking, chatting and laughing.

Arriving home, her absence hit me. I missed her. She was not waiting for me inside the door, ready for her supper; she did not jump through the window, having observed my return home from under a car or from the top of a wall. She did not claim her supper; she did not sleep on my bed.

I noticed the piece of string which was our favourite toy. I felt my eyes filling with tears. I thought: 'I shall never see Tsi-Tsa again.' I was crying.

Suddenly I felt very emotional; but this feeling was overshadowed by others: I felt angry with myself and deeply ashamed. When did I last cry? When my mother died, nine years before. Hedy, my sister, died in 1973. I loved her dearly, as much as I loved anyone in this world, but I did not cry. Having heard the news of B's death I felt sorry, and made the right, sympathetic noises and changed the subject. B lived in Budapest, I lived in London. He was a rubric in my life: I knew that in faraway Budapest there lived a nice chap, once upon a time a dear and close friend of mine, now a national figure whose picture I could often see in the Hungarian theatrical magazines. Our lives had moved into different orbits. While Tsi-Tsa was part of my everyday life. She slept on my bed when she deigned to do so; she claimed her food when she was hungry; she accompanied me to the shops and

75

waited for me outside, under a car or on the top of one. She was dependent on me.

All the same, I had to ask myself: what sort of monster was I? I took the news of B's death with conventional aloofness; I had not been over-emotional even over my sister's slow and painful death. And now, at the age of sixty-five, I was crying over the death or disappearance of my cat, formerly my half-cat.

I was livid with myself. Not only a monster but worse: a fool. I had always been irritated by all that sentimental rubbish about cats. I had always made fun, most contemptuously, of the silly English cat-worship, and now I was behaving . . . well, if anyone had told me this story about myself I would have refused to believe it.

But it was of no use. I always try to reason with my emotions. Amazingly, I often win such arguments. But not this time. I kept telling myself: 'I shall never see Tsi-Tsa again.' And nothing else mattered.

I had often said, when asked, that yes, I was living alone. Suddenly I realised that I had not lived alone. I had lived with Tsi-Tsa. I looked at the window, hoping for a miracle. But the curtain failed to hustle.

Now I was living alone.

*   *   *

Next day I felt an urge to *do* something. But what could I do? I rushed to the nearest newsagent and put up an ad in the window, promising a reward for proper information about Tsi-Tsa.

76

My wife Lea phoned. We live apart but are on very good terms. She told me that she had mentioned Tsi-Tsa's disappearance to a friend of hers, a great expert on cats, and her friend had told her that spoilt cats, when left alone, get terribly depressed, wander away and then are often taken in by strangers who think they are strays. But they do return eventually. It may take years but they return.

I phoned May. The story I heard from her was most upsetting. She told me that Tsi-Tsa started turning up on her doorstep. (Obviously, cats have longer memories than we presume. Now that Tsi-Tsa needed May, she remembered her all right.)

'I didn't let her in,' she said, 'because I did not want to start that two-homes business all over again. But she kept coming. Ricky, my son, suggested that you might be away. I said that was impossible because you would have told me. Who else would look after Sooty? One morning at six o'clock, I found her miaowing desperately on my doorstep. I still didn't let her in. I never thought you would go away without letting me know.'

It was becoming clearer now. Tsi-Tsa used to be the most spoilt cat in Fulham. Suddenly she felt abandoned by me, went back to her former home and was rejected once again. She must have been heart-broken and wandered away.

'What can I do now?' I asked May, a sensible woman who knew a great deal about cats.

'You must look for her.'

'Look for her? How can you look for a cat in a town with ten million people and five million cats?'

'The town is large but she is, after all, unlikely to

77

have gone to Highgate or Ilford. She can't be far
away.'

'But what if she's dead.'

'Then you won't find her.'

'One man against London, in search of a cat' I
thought. Then I spat. I felt disgusted with myself.
Tsi-Tsa was reducing me to an idiot. After outbursts
of sentimentality, this wave of self-pity. But I could
not convince myself to take the matter lightly.

In the afternoon I set out in search of Tsi-Tsa. We
went – a friend accompanied me – north, away from
Fulham Road, because I knew Tsi-Tsa would not
cross the main road. Fulham is full of cats. Any day I
walked a few minutes, I saw dozens of them. Today in
the first half hour we failed to spot one single cat.

'Look!' my friend shouted.

There was a black cat, sitting on a hut, on top of a
pile of old and broken furniture. I looked at the cat,
the cat looked at me. I failed to recognize her. Her face
looked arrogant and enigmatic. I went nearer, she
walked away slowly. I knocked on the door and a
woman opened it. Yes, the black cat was hers, in fact,
she had four of them. She adored black cats. No, she
did not care for cats of any other colour. They had to
be black. When I told her that I had lost not only a cat
but a black cat she became most sympathetic. She
took my name and telephone number and promised
that should she see an unknown black cat she would
ring me up.

This was the first taste of how Fulham would take
the loss of Tsi-Tsa. I thought people would shrug
their shoulders. 'Too bad. But how d'you expect to
find her? And what the hell can *I* do about it?' Not at

all. Tsi-Tsa's disappearance became public concern. After the Queen's Jubilee – in a few days – it seemed to be the most important event.

We walked on, looking for black cats, until we came to a newsagent. My friend needed some paper hankies, so in we went. She suggested that I should put up another advertisement. The more the better. I wrote out another ad, promising a reward and handed the note to the shopkeeper. I asked him how much I owed him.

'25 p.'

'But you said that was the price of the paper hankies. What about the advertisement?'

'I've read it. I won't charge for it.'

'But that's your livelihood.'

'That's the way I run my business. I charge for commercial ads but I refuse to make money on other people's misery.'

'In that case,' I told him, 'there's nothing else left to me but to thank you . . .'

I could not finish the sentence. My voice broke and my eyes were full of tears.

Good God. I was getting senile. What's happening to me? Where is the cynic? Where is the humorist? Oh, that bloody cat.

*　　*　　*

That evening I saw a black cat sitting on the fence of my patio. I went out; it ran away. Was it Tsi-Tsa? I could not be sure. As it was twice Tsi-Tsa's size, this seemed unlikely. But she could have put on weight. Perhaps it was Tsi-Tsa, toying with the idea of coming back but when she saw me, she remembered the misery I had caused her and ran away. I could not be sure.

Another friend rang me, gave me a lot of unsolicited advice and finished off by saying: 'Buy yourself another cat.'

Other people suggested the same thing. I failed to understand their mentality. I remembered an old story I had heard many years before about Gyula Csortos. He was a great actor, a true giant of the Budapest stage but a bitter and unpleasant man, a real misanthrope who loved only two living beings: his mother and his dog. With his dog he lived; with his mother he lunched every Wednesday.

One Tuesday Csortos's dog died. He was heartbroken. A big man, famous for his ice-cold sarcasm and complete lack of emotion, he now cried like a teenage girl. Next day his mother tried to console him:

'You must not take it *so* much to your heart, Gyula,' she said. 'In a few days you'll go and buy yourself another little dog . . .'

Csortos looked at her with murderous eyes: 'And when *you* die I'll go and buy myself another little old woman.'

*   *   *

I went out late at night for another search. I was concerned about Tsi-Tsa but was even more concerned about my own weakness and silliness. So I started rationalising. I was less upset about the death of B than about the disappearance of Tsi-Tsa because I *knew* that B was dead. Death is final. There is no appeal against it. But Tsi-Tsa may be alive. There is hope.

Then I was suddenly overcome by fury. I was maddened by anger. She may have felt rejected but now *I* felt rejected by her. There should be mutual affection between us. She had every right to make a point. Now she has made it. If she is alive why the hell doesn't she come back? She knows my address; I don't know hers.

*   *   *

On Tuesday, May advised me to go south in search of Tsi-Tsa.

'But you said she never crossed Fulham Road,' I told her.

'She was distressed. Perhaps she did this time.'

I trusted May's wisdom about cats, so I crossed Fulham Road. In Fulham Park Gardens I saw two young women get into a Mini. I asked them – somewhat mechanically, being fully aware of the hopelessness of the enquiry – if they had seen a little black cat. They showed great interest. No, they had not themselves seen a black cat, but a few days before a little girl was going from house to house, asking people if they had lost a black cat because her mother had found one. This sounded unbelievable, too good to be true. May was a witch, perhaps. She had sent me in this direction and now my very first enquiry seemed to bear fruit. Who was the little girl? Sorry, that they did not know. Whereabouts did she live? They did not know. She had long black hair and was about eight and, obviously, could not live very far away. Yes, if she called again or they saw her in the street they would talk to her and would give me a ring immediately. I am sure that having found out that much, James Bond would have found it child's play to unravel the whole mystery. But what could *I* do? I went from house to house, hoping that the little girl had called on others, too, and perhaps someone knew who she was. A few people did remember her call but no one knew where she lived.

A woman gave me a tip: 'There's a children's Jubilee Party at the Council Estate. The little girl might be there.'

I trotted to the Council Estate where the children's Jubilee Party was in full swing. A woman in a white jacket was organising everything and at this moment she was instructing the children to gather on a balcony to be photographed. The picture-taking took an interminably long time but as soon as it was over the Lady in White told my story to the whole gathering and asked if the little girl who had found the black cat was present. She was not.

I was about to leave when someone led me to Mrs Baines. I was told that all lost cats in the neighbourhood went straight to Mrs Baines. I repeated my story but she shook her head: 'No. Your cat is not around here.'

Was she sure? Quite sure. Did she know all the cats of Fulham? No, certainly not. But she did know all the *lost* cats of Fulham. Without exception? Yes, without exception. Every lost, abandoned or otherwise betrayed cat in SW6 always went straight to her. But how did the cats know her address? This was the cats' secret, but they did know. To make a long story short: she was absolutely certain that my cat was not around.

What about the little girl's story? Whatever the case, that black cat was not my black cat.

I went on, from house to house, from street to street. Nearly everyone reassured me that my cat would be found, but they could give me no information. Soon I realised that the Queen, naturally, was in the centre of their interest – but immediately after her came my cat. Strange people stopped me in the street: 'Have you found your cat yet?' Others rang my bell, carrying cats of varying size and varying

blackness. Others again called on me, reporting that they had seen a black cat somewhere not far.

Some of my experiences during these long days of search were not so touching.

One day a lady came to my door and reported that a black cat had been spotted at Ricmer Avenue, a nearby street to the north of us. We rushed there together. Yes, a black cat was sitting on a low wall. I picked it up and gave it a good look. It could be Tsi-

Tsa. And it could be another cat. I was lost. A very angry man came out of the house.

'What are you doing with my cat?' he shouted at me.

'Well, if it is your cat . . .'

'It is.'

'How long have you had him?'

'Her.'

'How long have you had her?'

'Six years. Long enough?'

The lady who had called me out, whispered: 'Nasty.'

'My cat has disappeared,' I started explaining.

'Everybody knows that.'

'Well, in that case . . .'

'In that case you want to get hold of another black cat. Put my cat down.' And he took a few menacing steps towards me.

I felt like a cat-thief. I meant to tell him the story about Csortos, his mother and his dog but I did not.

The other incident happened on the other side of Fulham Road. Someone pointed out a house, telling me that the man who lived there was a mentor of stray cats, he looked after lots of them.

I found the man in his front garden, tending his roses. I asked him if he had seen a little black cat.

'Probably. They come in all colours.'

'Would you be able to catch her if you see her again?'

'I wish I could.'

'If you *can* catch my cat, a little black one . . .'

He interrupted me:

'If I catch your little black cat I'll wring his neck.'

'Hers.'

'I'll wring her neck. That's what I always do with all of them.'

'I was told you liked cats.'

'I love them. But they don't like me. For some reason, all the bloody cats of Fulham – and quite a lot from Chelsea and a few odd ones from Putney – come to shit in my back garden. I don't know why they honour me but they do. They come in dozens, in scores, in hundreds, they have turned my beautiful garden into a gigantic cats' lavatory, they have ruined my flowers and made a frightful mess. If I catch your cat – that little black one – I'll wring her neck and I'll do it with special pleasure.'

For a moment I thought I'd point out to him the advantages of free manure but I desisted. I broke off negotiations. This did not seem a fruitful line of enquiry.

*　　*　　*

I went out to do some shopping. I went to Eddie's Polish delicatessen shop. Danka, his niece, started serving me but when Eddie heard my voice, he came out from the office and told me: 'Your cat keeps going to the butcher next door.'

I left everything and went over to Harry, the butcher.

'Are you talking of that little black female?'

Even in my excitement I could not help asking him: 'How do you know she's a female?'

'I looked at her. Can't you tell a boy from a girl?'

'When they are naked. When they both wear jeans and long hair, no.'

86

'Your cat was naked,' he said firmly. 'She keeps coming in. She is very miserable and hungry. I give her minced meat. If I had known she was your cat I would've caught her. I'll catch her next time.'

'She will run away.'

'Not from me.'

'She may not come again.'

'She will. By the way, do you know where she lives nowadays?'

'No idea.'

'Down in the alleyway.'

He showed me the alleyway, opening from Waldemar Avenue, the first parallel street to mine. I went through the narrow passage and came to the end. There was a tabby cat in the last house. The front of these houses looked at Fulham Road and in one of the houses there was an art gallery. I went round. The gallery was run by a charming young couple who owned the tabby cat. They told me that during the last few days a frightened and hungry black cat had, indeed, often appeared there, and she kept coming back. I asked them if they could catch her next time. No, she was too frightened and too wild. It was impossible to catch her. But they would call me next time they saw her. Hardly did I get home, when the phone rang. The black cat was in the alleyway. Half a minute later, I was there. I did not know that I could still run as fast as that. But it was not fast enough. Ten seconds before my arrival, I was told, the black cat had been frightened by a large male cat and ran away, across the back gardens. I went back to the alleyway twenty times a day. No sign of Tsi-Tsa, if indeed Tsi-Tsa was the mysterious black cat. I got a number of other phone calls from the gallery, I ran faster and faster but was always late.

I met May in the street.

'I've seen Sooty,' she told me.

'Where?'

'In front of our house.'

'You are sure it was Tsi-Tsa . . . I mean Sooty?'

'What d'you mean I'm sure? Of course I'm sure. My husband also saw her. He is sure, too. I called her and she came to me. But when I wanted to pick her up she ran away. She is frightened and very wild. But it was Sooty all right.'

I was deeply hurt. If she was in front of May's house, then she passed the corner of my street and she was no more than twenty yards away from my door. And she did not call. She did not look me up.

'I hope you'll catch her,' said May.

'I'm not interested any more.'

*   *   *

At 10.15 a.m. on Tuesday, June 14, the telephone rang. It was Harry, the butcher.

'I've got your cat.'

A minute later I was in the butcher's shop. Harry was serving a woman. He looked up: 'She's in the cellar.'

Tony, Harry's son took me down. It was a large and bright cellar, full of the carcasses of lambs and oxen, hanging on hooks. There was a little cat, hiding timidly in a corner, trembling and terrified. I picked her up. She showed no sign of recognition but did not resist.

Half way home the cat started a violent struggle and made a terrific effort to run away. Opening the door with one hand and holding this violently struggling animal with the other was quite a task but we reached the inside of the house all right. I threw her on the floor. She rushed to a corner and hid herself under the bookshelf – a place she had never frequented before.

She still showed no sign of recognition; neither did I.

I must explain that as some people are colour-blind, I am face-blind. I remember names without difficulty, I remember persons, encounters, conversations but not faces. I must see a person twenty-five times before I start recognising him and even then, I would recognise him more by his voice, manner of speaking, accent or some clue he gave me ('Have you seen the Shackletons lately?') than by his face. In my club I have some intimate friends. I know everything about them, their incomes, the secrets of their married life, their clandestine affairs – everything, except who they are. After years of intimate friendship I cannot possibly ask. Not even a common

89

friend, because he might start wondering whether I knew *his* name.

Once I had lunch with a member whom I immediately recognised as Lord Gardiner, the former Lord Chancellor. He turned out to be Laurence Olivier. I was truly shaken. Not recognising one of the best known faces in the country, which I had seen hundreds of times, was going a little too far even for me. But worse was to come. I flew to Zurich with a group, on some film-business, and we were accompanied by a young Swissair official. We knew that Peter S, from the Swiss National Tourist Office, would meet us at the airport and the Swissair man was anxious to meet him. When we were taxiing towards the airport building, we noticed two men in macintoshes on the tarmac.

'Is either of these Peter S?' asked the Swissair chap.

I ought to have told him that I was the last person to ask such a question. But I was sitting by the window and could give the two men a thorough look. I examined them carefully. I knew that Peter S was a small, fat man; these were both tall and slim. I gave another look to the two men and then declared:

'No. Neither is Peter S.'

Neither *was* Peter S. The one tiny detail which escaped my attention was that one of the two was my son, Martin.

Having failed to recognise my son, how could I be sure that I recognised my cat? Cat-faces are, after all, even more difficult than human faces. She was half her former size; she had been missing for exactly four weeks; her behaviour was utterly unlike her previous behaviour; her fur was rough; she showed no sign of having returned home. She hid herself in odd places, never frequented before, and showed no interest even in her plates (which had never been removed). Mrs Stangroom – the lady who helps to keep my house clean – had just arrived. She examined the cat.

'Are you our Pussy?' she asked, doubtfully.

The cat jumped off the sofa and hid herself under it.

'I don't think she is.'

I phoned Binky and asked him to come over. He examined the cat and shook his head: 'This cat is much smaller.'

'She's lost a lot of weight.'

'But she is just half of Tsi-Tsa's size.'

'Do you think she's Tsi-Tsa?'

'No, I don't.'

Good God. Is this cat going to stay here without my being sure who the hell she is? Tsi-Tsa or a stray? I phoned May. She was not at home but phoned me back after lunch. I told her about my predicament.

'Look at her ears.'

'Why?'

'Don't you know your own cat? She was in a fight when young and had one of her ears damaged.'

'The right or the left?'

'The right. But it may be the left.'

'Don't you know your own cat?' I asked her.

I told her that every cat had been in a fight when young and every cat had its ear damaged. Could she please come over and examine the extent, shape and character of the damage and thus identify Tsi-Tsa or dismiss her as an impostor.

She came. From the door she looked at Tsi-Tsa, still hiding under a chair. She said: 'Hallo Sooty.'

'Examine her ear.'

'I don't have to. It's Sooty all right.'

'You mean Tsi-Tsa?'

'No, I mean Sooty.'

But she did examine her ear.

'Oh yes. There's no doubt. It's Sooty all right.'

She left. I was far from convinced. It would be just like me to settle down with this cat, believing it was Tsi-Tsa, and then the real Tsi-Tsa would turn up eight months later as my wife's friend predicted.

Suddenly – as always when the excitement is over – I felt dead tired. I lay down on the sofa. I had gone through a lot because of this wretched cat (if this *was* the wretched cat). She had made me cry; she had made me feel a very painful sense of loss; I had been through the gamut of emotions; I had been sad, I had been inconsolable, I had been furious, I had felt rejected, I had been indifferent. I was ashamed of myself, perhaps a silly reaction but I *was* ashamed that a cat should reduce me to a sentimental old fool. At the same time I was also pleased. It seemed, that after all I was capable of some human emotions. I had rather doubted this. I may or may not have found Tsi-Tsa; but I felt that I had found myself. On the other hand, I thought, if this *was* myself, I ought to lose it again.

I fell asleep. When I woke up, Tsi-Tsa was lying on my chest, with her right paw on my left shoulder, half embracing me, as used to be her habit.

I had no more doubts. It was Tsi-Tsa all right.

And Again

FOR three days I kept Tsi-Tsa indoors. On the fourth day I opened the door for the postman and she shot out like the devil and disappeared before I could say Jack Robinson. But in an hour's time she not only returned but came back through the window, thus giving me the final proof of her true identity.

Her quick return reassured me that she could be safely let out. So I let her out whereupon she disappeared again. Two hours passed, four hours and a whole night. No sign of Tsi-Tsa.

'Damn,' I said but failed to get worked up. Not because I had grown less fond of her. But there is just so much of worrying capacity within me and I had spent it all in the last few weeks. Besides, I knew she was alive and kicking and knew she could not be far away.

Next morning the phone rang and a female voice asked: 'Have you found your cat yet?'

'Not only that I've found her,' I replied, but 'I've lost her again.'

'She's with me.' The voice gave me an address in Munster Road, the second parallel street to mine.

I walked over. A little girl opened the door and called her mother.

'I'll get her for you,' said the mother. 'She's in the outside loo. I couldn't keep her in the house because my own cat would've eaten her up.'

She told me that the previous night she and her husband came home late and they found Tsi-Tsa on the doorstep, frightened and forlorn, shivering and unhappy. She took her in, fed her and locked her in the loo.

'But how did you know my telephone number?'

'Early this morning I went to the hairdresser and it was then that I saw your ad at the newsagent's window.'

This was the newsagent who had refused to accept money for the advertisement. He was pleased when I told him later how effective his kind service was.

I went to buy a collar for Tsi-Tsa and asked the pet-shop owner to engrave her name and telephone number on a disc. And asked him to remove the little bell from the red collar.

'But why?' he protested.

'Because with the bell on she won't be able to catch birds.'

He was shocked. I did not really quite mean it. I was not too pleased when Tsi-Tsa, from time to time, came through the window with a little bird in her mouth whom, later, she devoured completely, lock stock and barrel, feathers, claws and all. But at least Tsi-Tsa obeyed feline nature while people who go out and shoot birds for sheer pleasure in their thousands, do not just obey human nature. I felt it cruel to compel an animal to live with a bell on her neck and ring it with every step. A cow may like it – although I doubt it; a cat must hate it. And I have heard that

while the bell drives the cats crazy, it does not impede their ability to catch birds.

This second disappearance was Tsi-Tsa's last. Perhaps that night in the outside loo was the last straw for her. She settled down and became her former impudent, arrogant self again. She sat in the window, surveying the street with imperious superciliousness, accepting the smiles or adulation of passers-by with lofty disdain. She accompanied me on my shopping expeditions, slept on my chest with her right paw on my left shoulder, she sat on my lap for hours, we played together with that piece of string on the top of the stairs and she went on slapping Ginger's face with ferocious wickedness whenever Ginger ventured into the house. Ginger was a twice-a-day visitor, accepted the slaps more in sorrow than in anger, then walked, slowly and thoughtfully, to Tsi-Tsa's plate and ate up her food.

Tsi-Tsa, being a great beauty, was loved and admired by the human population of Fulham and being a solitary type, conceited and jealous, was universally detested by her fellow-cats.

But the excitements were over and we settled down to a peaceful and uneventful life. For a very short while.

A Happy Event?

*　　*　　*

UNTIL Tsi-Tsa got pregnant.

Soon after she returned, I noticed that she was growing fat. I made some remarks upon her size but my friends laughed.

'Of course she's getting fat. You've always spoilt and overfed her but since you and Tsi-Tsa were reunited you've become even worse. She's eating too much so she's getting fat. Simple as that.'

But she was getting much too fat for just ordinary putting on weight. She developed an enormous belly and the inevitable proposition slowly dawned on me that she was pregnant. But she couldn't be pregnant.

There were a few women chatting on the other side of the road, opposite my house. All great cat-lovers and experts. I joined their group.

'My cat seems to be pregnant,' I told them.

They burst out laughing: '*Seems?*'

But however loud they laughed, it was impossible: she could not be pregnant. She had been spayed, May had told me quite clearly. By now I had known Tsi-Tsa for five years. She certainly would have produced kittens – twice a year, in fact – if she had not been spayed.

'Sometimes it happens,' said one of the Wise

Women of Fulham, 'that the job is not done properly and the cat starts having kittens after a while.'

But how long is a 'while'? Five years or more? Maybe.

Numerous and diverse views were expressed. May told me once again that Tsi-Tsa had been neutered, she could not be pregnant and that was that. Lea, my wife, knows little about cats but is a good observer and has a great deal of common sense. She declared that there was no doubt about it: Tsi-Tsa *was* pregnant. Sonia, my painter-friend from Berlin, an ardent admirer of Tsi-Tsa, was in London and she approached the matter pragmatically. She would find out – she said. Someone told her that if Tsi-Tsa *was* pregnant then, by now – judging by her size – there must be concrete signs of her pregnancy: should one touch her tummy gently one ought to feel movements inside. So she settled down to experiment. She touched Tsi-Tsa's tummy extremely gently and told me that yes, she definitely felt movement inside. Then she repeated the experiment and this time she felt nothing. Then she felt it again, then she didn't. In the end she came to a considered opinion: 'I don't know,' she said.

Two Jehovah's Witnesses knocked on my door and tried to sell me their magazine, *Watch Tower*. I bought a copy in order to get rid of them but they wanted to come in to explain its contents to me and convert me to Jehovah Witnessism. I told them that I had no time, I was busy with much weightier affairs. Weightier than my soul? Much weightier, I replied, and told them my predicament about Tsi-Tsa. Was she pregnant or wasn't she pregnant? And if she was, what was the explanation? How did a spayed cat become pregnant?

One of the Jehovah's Witnesses, a thin and tall Englishwoman (the other was a black lady), walked to Tsi-Tsa, examined her and declared firmly: 'There can be no possible doubt: your cat *is* pregnant. And the explanation is simple: a miracle has occurred.'

This seemed to be the likeliest explanation to date. As I was afraid that the next step would be that the lady would develop a theory of immaculate conception by Tsi-Tsa, I bought another *Watch Tower* and said goodbye to them. Mrs Stangroom (the lady who helps to clean my house) had a more earthy but more worrying theory: 'She's not our pussy. I always knew she wasn't.'

A crisis of identity was added to the other crises. I was convinced she *was* our pussy. I recognised many of her ways, habits, mannerisms and had no doubt whatsoever about her identity. But I had made mistakes before. And I knew that the more certain you feel about something the more sceptical you ought to be. It all boiled down to this: if she was Tsi-Tsa, how could she be pregnant? If she wasn't Tsi-Tsa, who the hell was she?

But like all problems of identity this, too, was a false one. The Csortos theory did not apply. It was not important whether she was Tsi-Tsa or I got 'another little cat' instead. I accepted her as Tsi-Tsa; I treated her as Tsi-Tsa; I loved her as my Tsi-Tsa, so far as I was concerned, she was my Tsi-Tsa whoever else she may have been.

Tsi-Tsa, as I recalled it now, showed no amorous tendencies and kept all cats – suitors as well as other females – at a distance. But nowadays she had started going out more and more. She stayed away for hours on end. On one occasion she stayed away for the night. But it was, after all, useless to ponder over this problem. She had spent a whole month on her own and if her morals weakened, they weakened during her absence.

I came to two conclusions.

First: If Tsi-Tsa was pregnant, she should be treated with affection and understanding. Her kittens

should be treated like members of the family. To kill a kitten was absolutely out of the question. How many does a cat produce? Four? Five? I shall try to place some with respectable families, in good homes. The rest will have to be kept. I was far from overjoyed. I did not mind a cat but did not want a cattery. But Tsi-Tsa would be even less pleased. She would be madly jealous even of her own offspring.

Second: there was a simple way of finding out whether Tsi-Tsa was pregnant or not. Not to ask the Wise Women of Fulham; not to rely on Sonia's experiments; not to believe in miracles. But to consult a vet. So I rang one up not far from me and his secretary told me to come along on Wednesday afternoon at five past five. Not at five o'clock but at five past five. She was cutting it fine, I thought, not knowing how busy vets were and, indeed, that often they spent less than two minutes on a patient. Even to make an appointment for seven minutes and thirty-eight seconds past five would have been quite reasonable.

After lunch, on Wednesday, I tried hard to work but my phone kept ringing. And there was another thing which prevented me from concentrating on what I was doing: Tsi-Tsa was not around. She went out in the morning and failed to return by one. No sign of her at two. At three. Just like that bloody cat: she's never around when she is wanted. We shall be late at the vet. We'll come at eight minutes past five and will have missed our turn.

At half past four the telephone rang.

'Tanners of Fulham,' a voice said.

That is the show-room almost next door to me, on the opposite side of Fulham Road. I had never had any dealings with them. It flashed through my mind that they must have heard about the burning of my car and were trying now to sell me a new one. I buy my suits at Moss Bros, twenty yards from the Garrick Club to the right as you come out; I bought my new car at Renaults, twenty yards away from the Garrick on the left. Moss Bros would be happy if people chose suits as quickly and with as little fuss as I chose my car. But anyway, I bought that car two days after the explosion, so the car-people were too late. I remembered now that a few days before they had left a message on my telephone answering machine – they certainly did persevere.

'Tanners of Fulham,' the voice said.

'Yes?'

Their call was not about a car; it was about Tsi-Tsa.

'Do you have a little black cat?'

'I do.'

'She has just been run over by a car in front of our shop.'

Touch and Go

*   *   *

I RAN across Fulham Road so carelessly that I was nearly run over myself.

There was Tsi-Tsa, lying on the pavement, not crying or whimpering but obviously in great pain. There was some horrible-looking brownish-red liquid around her, probably blood mixed with other stuff. But she was alive and without external injuries. She was blinking and terrified but uttered no sound. She looked up when I arrived, she could move her head and her front paws but, so it seemed, not her hind legs.

'She will have to be destroyed,' said one of the small group of strangers surrounding her. The man spoke with apparent relish, he was glad that a cat would have to be destroyed. He continued: 'Her spine is broken. Watch, she can't move her hind legs.'

I watched. She moved her hind legs. Very slowly and with great difficulty but she moved them.

'The RSPCA ambulance's been called,' another spectator informed me.

A girl of about twenty was crouching next to Tsi-Tsa, trying to comfort her. She was affectionate and greatly distressed.

A salesman from Tanners told me what had

happened. Tsi-Tsa had got into the habit of visiting the show-room. Apparently, after her disappearance, she became bolder and ventured to cross Fulham Road. When a kitten, still with May – the reader may recall – she was knocked over on the Fulham Road by a car, almost at the same spot as now. For years she never crossed Fulham Road again. But she grew fond of the show-room. People liked her; she sat on the top of the cars; when she found one open, she got inside; occasionally she jumped onto clients' laps when they were sitting opposite the salesmen, negotiating a deal. One night she was locked into the show-room – no one noticed that she was sleeping in a car – and that was the night when she failed to turn up at home. Another evening she was locked in again but one of the salesmen returned to the shop at midnight, heard her crying and let her out. Next day this salesman tried to phone me (Tsi-Tsa's number was now on the disc of her collar) but I failed to ring back.

That morning (the date was 28 September 1977) she spent a few hours in the show-room and she was on her way home when the accident happened. There were two people in a white car, driven by a learner driver.

'He had plenty of time to stop,' the man who had decreed that Tsi-Tsa was to be destroyed informed me. 'Any other driver could do it. Bad luck.'

'Always these bloody learners,' a thin woman commented. Scapegoats must always be found. She sounded as if learner drivers were the source of all evil on this planet.

The learner drove on towards the West End, without stopping. Two young men who had witnessed the scene, jumped into their car and pursued him. They reached the white car at Fulham Broadway.

'I told the driver,' one of the young men told me, 'that he had hit a cat. Perhaps killed it.'

'What did he reply?'

'That he didn't care,'

A man asked: 'Do you have his registration number?'

'Yeah.'

'What it is?'

'I won't tell you. What's the point?'

He was right, what was the point? First, I wanted to concentrate on Tsi-Tsa and not prosecuting learner drivers. Second, he had committed no offence. You must stop after hitting a dog. But cats do not count, you may drive on.

The young girl, crouching by Tsi-Tsa, who had not spoken till then, said in a quiet but passionate voice: 'I would prosecute.'

'Why?' someone asked her.

'To teach people that they cannot run over animals and get away with it.'

But they can.

The RSPCA ambulance had not turned up so I came home and phoned them up. Yes, they knew of the accident and the man was on his way. I went back to Tsi-Tsa and the ambulance had, in fact, arrived in the meantime.

The driver was kind and helpful. I thought he was a trained animal nurse and, in my own need for comfort, treated him as an oracle. I asked him what seemed to be wrong with Tsi-Tsa but he refused to comment. A vet must see her first. I mentioned her pregnancy.

'Oh yes,' said the driver, 'it's quite common that a few years after an operation, if it wasn't properly performed, a cat gets pregnant again. But when a cat is pregnant there are other signs, too. You must have observed them.'

Other signs? Yes, I did observe them. Now that he mentioned them, the whole thing became clear. Tsi-Tsa had become much more affectionate in the last few weeks. She jumped onto everybody's lap – a thing she had not done before. She started looking into dark corners and now I realised that she must have been looking for a place to deliver her first children. I had decided to buy a comfortable basket for her as soon as the vet confirmed her pregnancy. She would not need it now. She must have lost her kittens. But the driver was right. Everything fitted into the picture perfectly.

It was twenty-two minutes after five. The driver told me to ring the hospital at six and drove off with Tsi-Tsa.

During these thirty-eight minutes I realised that I was less upset than after Tsi-Tsa's disappearance. That seemed strange. While she was away, she could have been dead or alive – I had no means of knowing – but, in the end, she turned up in perfect health. Now I *knew* that she had been badly hurt and her life was in danger. But I was less upset because I was not responsible. My guilt or innocence was, apparently, more important than Tsi-Tsa's life or death.

* * *

I phoned the hospital at six. I was told that she almost certainly had a broken pelvis. She was being X-rayed now. I asked what a broken pelvis meant from the point of view of survival.

'The broken pelvis will probably heal,' the nurse replied. 'But we are worried about many other things. Please ring in an hour's time.'

I did and this time I talked to a woman vet. Tsi-Tsa had been X-rayed and it was found that she had multiple fractures of her pelvis. This was serious but a

pelvis would heal. If that was all, she ought to be well again. But it was possible – indeed likely – that her spinal cord was injured, too. The X-ray could not show that and it would take four or five days before they could be sure.

'And there are further complications,' she added.

'The pregnancy?' I asked.

'What pregnancy?'

I explained.

'I examined her for fractures, not for pregnancy,' she said. 'But when we X-ray the spine, the abdomen shows, too. Wait, I'll have a look.'

I waited with bated breath. If she *was* pregnant, it was possible that she was not Tsi-Tsa. Would I prefer her to be a strange cat – I asked myself – now that she was probably dying?

The vet came back.

'No, she is not pregnant.'

'Why was she so fat then?'

'Middle-age and overfeeding.'

I remembered the driver's theory and my recollections about affection and her searching for a dark place for delivering her kittens. Everything fitted into the picture perfectly; but – as so often – it was the wrong picture.

I changed the subject: 'What are her chances for survival?'

'I was afraid you would ask that. I don't know. We'll see in four or five days.'

*   *   *

Two days later I realised that I had already betrayed Tsi-Tsa in my heart.

My old friend George Faludy wrote a moving, beautiful and brutal poem when his wife was dying of cancer. They spent some of her last weeks in Italy and he was upset and heartbroken. He loved his wife and knew that there was no way of fighting this horrible and destructive disease. But underneath their tender and mutual love there was burning and mutual hatred, too. She resented the fact that he would survive her and enjoy life when she was lying under the earth; and he dreamt of Venice. If she died quickly, he could go to see Venice once again, before the cold weather set in. It is sad that she must die; but as she must, why does she not hurry up and get on with it? We all have such cruel and ambivalent thoughts about people we love but Faludy, a great poet, had the honesty and courage to put them down. My predicament was different, of course. I wasn't about to lose a wife, only a cat. My temperament, my imagination, my despair did not match Faludy's. But I had betrayed Tsi-Tsa, all the same. I wanted her, of course, to get well. But what could I do? If she died, I would be freer; I wouldn't be tied to the house. I would be able to travel again. I wanted Tsi-Tsa to get well. But, on the other hand, I never really *wanted* a cat.

Was this callousness? Or just trying to prepare for the blow? Consoling myself in advance?

And what about that hypocrisy about Tsi-Tsa being 'only a cat'? Do we and should we value human beings, however hateful, above all animals, however lovable? To say that in a dramatic situation I would have preferred saving Tsi-Tsa to saving Adolf Hitler does not say much and not only because of the anachronism involved, as Tsi-Tsa was born a quarter of a century after Hitler's death. But Hitler was an extreme case so it does not really count. Besides, I cannot easily imagine a situation in which the dilemma could have arisen whether I wanted to save the Führer or Tsi-Tsa. But we all pay lip-service to the sanctity of human life while all humanity acts as if human life were cheap and valueless. What about animal life? Is human life regarded as more sacred just because we happen to be human and value ourselves, with unfounded conceit, above cats, horses and whales? These animals never speak of the sanctity of cat-life, horse-life and whale-life but – whatever their views on sanctity – never kill their own kind. Hand on your heart: in a fire, would you *always* prefer saving the life of your own worst enemy to saving your favourite dog?

*   *   *

Next morning at eleven I went to visit Tsi-Tsa in hospital. There are no visiting hours – the staff is too busy for that – but they are also kind and considerate and take you to the patient 'in justified cases'. The hospital was like all other hospitals except that the patients were animals. We had to wait a little (Sonia had come with me) and were then led into the ward. The nurse led us along a corridor and opened a door. One wall of one smallish room was covered with cages, each containing a sick cat. The nurse led us to one cage and there lay Tsi-Tsa. She was dazed – she must have been given pain-killer. She recognised me with greater assurance than I had recognised her after her return. The door of the cage was opened and Sonia stroked Tsi-Tsa's head. She was pleased but did not purr. We stayed a minute or two. When we were going out, Tsi-Tsa raised her head and followed us with her eyes until the door was shut behind us.

I asked the sister how Tsi-Tsa was.

'Her spine seems to be all right and that's decisively important. The fractures are bad but they will heal. The trouble is that we are not quite sure about internal injuries. It sometimes happens that after such accidents they cannot control their bowel movements. Then you cannot possibly keep her. And you should not, really, because her life would be utter misery. But let's keep our fingers crossed.'

On the way out I saw a price-list. Among other services painless destruction was advertised too. Euthanasia for cats is permitted. You can condemn your pet to death and it will be executed for £2.75.

*　　*　　*

Here are some of my notes, made during the days of Tsi-Tsa's illness:

SEPTEMBER 29 (the same day as the visit just described). Went to visit Tsi-Tsa again, late in the afternoon. They did not want to let me in but the receptionist took me to see her. She was heavily drugged. I stroked her feet through the rail. There was a vet's instruction, written on a small piece of paper: *Please inform me immediately if she passes faeces or urine.*

SEPTEMBER 30. Visited Tsi-Tsa at 6.30. She was much livelier, looked relaxed. No pain-killers. She had peed. General rejoicing. The nurse told me that she was not out of danger yet – far from it – but her prospects were brighter.

A friend told me that if she remains crippled I ought to 'put her to sleep'. I hate this euphemism. If she just limps a bit why should I condemn my little Tsi-Tsa to death? No. If it depends on me, Tsi-Tsa will live.

OCTOBER 1. Told by hospital not to go to see Tsi-Tsa because she was restive. Was this a good sign or a bad one? The nurse I was talking to could not say much but informed me that otherwise she was 'comfortable'. Just like any other hospital.

OCTOBER 3. Visited Tsi-Tsa. The Head Nurse came in with me and took her out of the cage. She did not like that and wanted to go back. Head Nurse said she was better than she dared hope. All bodily functions all right. If there is no relapse I could take her home in a week or two.

Head nurse also said that they get hospitalised, in other words get used to their cages and hate to be taken out.

SUNDAY, OCTOBER 9. Brought Tsi-Tsa home from hospital. She was brought out from the ward in a box. In the car she whined a bit.

She seems to be pleased to be at home but her limping is quite pathetic. She can hardly drag herself along. Every step is painful. Yet, when I opened the door of the house, she shot out at surprising speed. How she negotiated the step in front of the entrance I do not know. She could not do it on the way back, I had to lift her.

Quadratic Equations

*　　*　　*

'I DON'T really like writers,' a clever woman-friend once told me, 'because they keep observing you, collecting material. They always have an ulterior motive and try to fit you in, at least as a minor character, in their next book.'

'That goes only for novelists,' I replied. 'You may go on loving me.'

'How many novels have you written?'

'Three,' I admitted.

Touché, all right. True, I am not totally innocent of these charges. One day – quite recently – I drove out from my garage and Tsi-Tsa jumped away from the wheels in the last moment. As she cannot jump with breathtaking speed and agility, that last moment was a pretty close shave. I got a shock, but when I was driving away I caught myself thinking what a dramatic and unexpected end it would have given this book – on which I was working – if I had killed my own beloved cat. For a moment I actually regretted that I had not run her over.

That passing thought passed very quickly indeed. But there is no getting away from it: it *did* occur to me. On the other hand, to finish a story with such melodramatic, self-pitying, sentimental rubbish is

not to my taste. I had just read Graham Greene's new novel, *The Human Factor*. I quite liked it although I was far from overwhelmed. All the same, I felt fed up with spies and spy-stories. Spies are becoming horrible bores and they are quite unreal. I know they exist, indeed, there are too many of them. Too many spies keep chasing too few secrets. But the people we meet are not spies, they are chartered accountants, grocers, shoemakers, junior executives in machine-tool factories, lawyers and carpenters. The real drama of life is about love, jealousy, betrayal of personal trust, ambition, frustration, humiliation, anger and hatred and not – most definitely not – about murder, spies being chased, spies crossing frontiers disguised as blind men and escaping to Moscow. On reflection, I felt that Tsi-Tsa's story is, as it happened, more dramatic, more true and more human (if it is humanity one wishes to find in cats) than if it had ended in a dramatic death, with a Freudian murder.

After her return from the hospital, Tsi-Tsa was depressed for weeks. She realised that she could not do things she had been able to do before: she could not jump, she could not run, she could not get out through the window, she had to drag herself most pathetically from one point to another. She sat on the carpet, looked into empty space and lost interest in life. Very occasionally, she ventured out to the patio. Other cats were as cruel as children: they disliked her, were afraid of her disability and blamed her for it. We all feel repelled by cripples, but one of the achievements of civilisation is that we overcome this feeling or at least act as though we had overcome it. Cats – although very civilised in some respects – are not civilised enough in this one and made Tsi-Tsa's life even more miserable.

It was now that Ginger, the saint, performed a miracle. Tsi-Tsa did not attack him any more, she did not attack anyone. Ginger kept coming in, as before, and Tsi-Tsa watched him with slightly disapproving curiosity. But Ginger, a nobler soul than the rest, a former friend and patron of Beelzebub and other hungry, poor, stray cats, *felt* that Tsi-Tsa needed friendship and affection. So he gave it to her. He sat with her, was exquisitely polite to her, sought her company and, in a gentle and sophisticated way, even courted her. He wanted no favours from Tsi-Tsa but meant to give her back her self-respect and self-confidence. And he succeeded to a large extent.

Tsi-Tsa got used to Ginger, she seemed to like him now, she was pleased when he came in.

After a few weeks Tsi-Tsa started improving, both physically and mentally. She moved better now; she started coming up to the bedroom, negotiating the steps with increasing ease; she went out into the street, particularly when the sun was shining; she started playing with her favourite piece of string and occasionally even suggested a game of hide and seek.

She could not jump on to my bed or my lap but she pulled herself up with her front claws, thus scratching and wounding my legs and ruining my trousers. But I felt a few small wounds and a few pairs of trousers were a small price to pay for Tsi-Tsa's happiness.

Her philosophy was clear and I watched it crystallize in her mind. 'Very well, I shall have to live a limited life. Better than no life at all. I shall enjoy it. I shall adjust myself to the new circumstances and I shall be happy. Happiness, after all (added Tsi-Tsa) is a gift which you either have or don't have and it has very little to do with circumstances. I have the gift of happiness.'

I decided to take her to the vet – the same vet with whom we had to break an appointment on the day of the accident. I took Tsi-Tsa to the car in a box, knowing that she was unable to jump out of it. But *she* did not know that, so she jumped out of the box with the ease of a healthy kitten, hid herself under a car and giggled. There was not a soul in the street to help me. At last a girl came along but she was allergic to cats so she could not help. Then Ginger appeared, went under the car, probably just to say 'Hallo' to Tsi-Tsa but she moved out with the old, arrogant disdain. I caught her but we were fifteen minutes late.

The vet said that she had lost the use of the muscles in one of the hind legs. He started twisting her right leg as if Tsi-Tsa had been a toy cat and her leg made of wool. She failed to react, obviously felt nothing.

'To all intents and purposes,' said the vet, 'she is a three-legged cat now. I don't think she will improve although she might a little, very very slowly. But there is no reason why she should not reach a ripe old age.'

But Tsi-Tsa went on improving rather more quickly than anticipated. She can now run at staggering speed, although only for short distances. When getting up on to my lap, she uses her hind legs more and more, and the claws of her front paws less and less. The other day, to my utter amazement, she jumped out of the window, just like in the old days. But she must have been even more amazed by her own reckless audacity than I, because she did not attempt that feat again for a week. Then she leapt again. And again. And today she jumps out whenever she pleases. She cannot leap *up* to come back. Not yet.

Every morning the newspapers are thrown in at seven o'clock. Then Tsi-Tsa comes up to the bedroom – unless she is already there – jumps on the bed and settles down on my chest in her favourite pose. I stroke her head and try to go back to sleep. But she is purring too loudly and wants to be stroked, so she pushes her head under my hand. After a while I manage to go to sleep again and about half past eight I get up. She goes to the bathroom door and waits for me outside. Then she goes to the steps, lies down on the sixth step (out of seven) and I start to dangle the string in front of her. She makes one or two attempts to catch it but then turns and hurries down to her plates. It is the old, impudent Tsi-Tsa again. She is clearly telling me: 'All right, I'm playing this stupid, childish game with the string for your sake as you seem to be so fond of it. But enough is enough.' She gets her breakfast, eats half of it and goes to the door, to be let out. I open the door a few inches and Ginger rushes in like a tiger, leaping across Tsi-Tsa, runs to her plates and eats up what's left and drinks her milk. Tsi-Tsa looks back in sorrow, shakes her head and goes out. A little later she comes back and then both cats settle down under the table and sleep side by side.

Tsi-Tsa has shaken off her depression, adjusted herself to a new life and accepted her limitations with a kind of wisdom I have not often found in human friends. She cannot solve quadratic equations, knows very little about the later Roman Emperors and has no idea who Chomsky is. Her actual *knowledge* is limited; her wisdom is vast. When it comes to wisdom, she beats nearly all my friends (the majority of whom cannot solve quadratic equations either, know just as little about the later Roman Emperors as Tsi-Tsa does and have only the faintest idea who Chomsky is).

That's Tsi-Tsa's story. Her biography. While writing it, I was told several times by various friends that I was wasting my time.

'Cats come and go. Cats are born and die, leaving little trace behind and very few memories. What does it matter whether they lived or not?'

How true. Cats, in this respect, are just like human beings.